The Great Canadian Apple Cookbook

The Great Canadian Apple Cookbook

'Eh' is for Apple

Millview Publishing
Bath, Ontario

Published by:
Millview Publishing
P.O. Box 444
Bath, Ontario, Canada
K0H 1G0
millview@limestone.kosone.com

Canadian Cataloguing in Publication Data

Main entry under title:

The great Canadian apple cookbook: 'eh' is for apple

Includes index
ISBN No. 0-9684980-0-0

1. Cookery (Apples).
I. Boyd, G. David, 1945 - .

TX813.A6G73 1999 641.6'411 C99-930476-3

Printed and bound in Canada by Friesens, Altona, Manitoba.

Millview Publishing would like to thank the Ontario Apple Marketing Commission for supporting this publication.

Design and Page Composition: Victoria Boyd
Publishing Editor: G. David Boyd
Photographs: Victoria & David Boyd

This book proves that anything is possible
when you have found the right person.

Dedicated to Etta and George Boyd,
of Brentwood Bay, B.C.,
who, by demonstrating their mutual love,
inspired us.

Table of Contents

A Special Note of Thanks

The Ontario Apple Marketing Commission, representing Ontario's apple growers, is proud to assist in the publication of the first ever all-Canadian apple cookbook.

Realizing the importance of fruits and vegetables in the diets of Canadians, the apple growers of Ontario strongly support Canada's Food Guide to Healthy Eating. The Great Canadian Apple Cookbook is filled with recipes that will help you in attaining the recommended 5 to 10 servings of fruits and vegetables daily using Ontario apples.

Ontario's apple industry is steeped in tradition and is an important part of Ontario's economy. The use of Ontario apple varieties in cooking will support your local Ontario apple grower.

We want to thank David and Victoria Boyd for compiling this collection of recipes and offering us the opportunity of sponsoring the publication of this very special cookbook.
We hope you enjoy it.

Bon *apple*tit!

**ONTARIO
APPLE
MARKETING
COMMISSION**

Introduction – 'Eh' is for apple!

Take a moment to think back to your childhood and remember an apple-scented moment. Do you remember apple blossoms in the spring? Apple pie and ice cream? How about a chilly October evening, you and your friends all dressed as pirates, princesses, tramps, and monsters? Do you remember scampering through the neighbourhood, running from door to door calling out, "Trick or treat!" until you found a home where caramel apples were being handed out? The word quickly spread of the sweetest of Hallowe'en treats.

In the full heat of summer, or the languid days of September, at the local fair grounds, along the midway, there would be a garishly lit stall showcasing shiny, red candy apples. What a sticky, sugary treat!

You may recall the street vendors in places like Toronto. On Front Street, just outside Union Station, there they were, selling roasted chestnuts, popcorn and the ubiquitous taffy apples. They didn't cost more than fifteen cents and they were delicious. Golden brown, flattened on the bottom, where they rested on a neat square of wax paper.

If apple pies are your favourite memory, you might have had a thick piece served with a lovely wedge of old cheddar cheese or a drizzle of maple syrup -- or both! Or the very best of apple memories-- those apples picked from a neighbour's tree, (without permission of course!). We'd shine their red skins to a high gloss on our shirts and then turn the stems while reciting the alphabet; when it broke we'd know the first initial of the one were were destined to marry. With a home and a kitchen of my own, I still love apples, now, for more reasons than ever.

Canadians have a great advantage: we were growing apples on homesteads and in kitchen gardens long before Confederation in 1867. Since that time, we have learned that many everyday dishes can be enhanced by apples.

Canadian farmers continue to develop apple varieties, adding qualities that continue to ensure the apple as a perfect food. Join us in this celebration of a most versatile and delightful fruit.

McIntosh

~ Fresh Eating ~ Pies ~ Salads ~ Sauces ~

This truly Ontario variety originated in Eastern Ontario nearly 200 years ago, and has since spread all over North America and other parts of the world. A medium-sized apple, red in colour with a green background. The flesh is white. It's a juicy apple, crisp, becoming mild and nearly sweet when ripe. Very aromatic, the McIntosh has a delightful flavour – excellent for eating fresh. It can also be cooked in pies or made into sauce. The McIntosh is available from mid-September through to April or May from storage.

Red Delicious

~ Fresh Eating ~ Salads ~

There is no mistaking the look or the taste of a Red Delicious apple. It has an exclusive profile, a tapered shape with five distinct knobs on the bottom of the apple. Red Delicious can be dark red, brilliant red or sometimes light red with bold stripes and tinges of yellow. The flesh is creamy white and fine grained, sweet, crisp and juicy with a mild aroma. It's an excellent eating apple and should not be used for cooking. Available from October through to late Spring.

Varieties

Northern Spy

~ Pies ~ Baked ~ Sauces ~

Ontario grows a premium 'Northern Spy' apple and this is the apple for pies! This apple is large and red striped, with flesh that is yellowish and rather firm. Very juicy and tart. It is excellent for eating fresh but it is supreme for cooking. Available from October through to Spring months.

Empire

~ Fresh Eating ~ Salads ~ Sauces ~

The Empire is a relative newcomer, a cross of the McIntosh and Red Delicious which gives it a unique flavour. This apple is medium-sized and predominantly dark red, striped and blushed, contrasting with light yellow background. The flesh is juicy, cream-coloured, mild in flavour and sweet. It's a high-quality dessert type for eating fresh and also cooks well. Available from early October until early summer.

Idared

~ Fresh Eating ~ Pies ~ Baked ~

A late season varicty, a cross of the Jonathon and Wagener varieties. A medium to large apple, uniform in shape and solid bright red. The flesh of the Idared is firm and white and somewhat acid. A late keeping apple, it is good for eating and cooking. Although tart at picking time it mellows with storage. This apple tastes best after Christmas. This variety is available from October to August.

Cortland

~ Fresh Eating ~ Pies ~ Salads ~ Sauces ~

A cross between the McIntosh and Ben Davis varieties, the Cortland is a medim to large apple, and somewhat flat oval in shape. It is bright red with a green/yellow cheek. The flesh is snow white and quite firm. It is mildly tart and delicate in texture. When cut it retains its white colour longer than any other variety, making it especially good for salads and fruit cups. Good for eating and a good baking apple for apple pies and sauces. Available from October to February.

Spartan

~ Fresh Eating ~ Pies ~ Salads ~

A medium-sized apple of a red variety produced by crossing McIntosh with Newton. The Spartan has a sweet, distinctive flavour, crisp white flesh and an unusually small core. A good eating and cooking apple. Available from October through early summer.

Golden Delicious

~ Fresh Eating ~ Pies ~ Baked ~ Sauces ~

A yellow apple, sometimes greenish yellow and generally medium to large in size. The flesh has a yellowish tinge, fine grained and mildly aromatic, crisp and tender. The Golden Delicious tastes sweet and juicy. An all-purpose apple, good for eating and cooking. Available October to January.

Varieties

Cripin/Mutsu

~ Fresh Eating ~ Pies ~ Salads ~

A cross between the Golden Delicious and the Indo varieties. The name tells its Japanese origin. This is a large apple, which can be green or yellow at maturity, sometimes with an orange blush. The flesh is firm very dense in texture and juicy. Excellent for eating fresh and for baking. Available from late October through to April.

Russett

~ Fresh Eating ~ Pies ~ Sauces ~

An old acquaintance that has won a renewal of interest. The Golden Russett is a medium to small apple, golden brown, with a rusty skin. The flesh is firm, yellowish, fine grained and aromatic, excellent for eating fresh. Available from November through to April.

Gala

~ Fresh Eating ~

A cross of Kidd's Orange and Golden Delicious from New Zealand. Gala is a promising new apple maturing in September. Fruit size is medium and of excellent quality. Gala has rated very well in a number of taste panels. It is a striped red apple that frequently shows a complex red surface with white flecks muted by a hazy, waxy appearance, yet it is very attractive. Available during McIntosh season or earlier.

Jonagold

~ Fresh Eating ~ Pies ~ Baked ~ Sauces ~

This apple originated from Geneva, NY, as a Golden Delicious crossed with Jonathon. It is very popular in Europe and is gaining importance in North America because of its high quality and flavour. Jonagold is a large apple with an attractive orangish-red blush and a slight hint of a stripe over a beautiful yellow ground colour. Excellent for fresh use and cooking.

And they're good for you!

Nutrition Information

per 138 g serving (one medium)

Energy	82 Cal 341 kJ
Protein	0.26 g
Fat	0.5 g
Carbohydrate	21.1 g
Dietary Fiber	5.2 g
Sodium	0 mg
Potassium	159 mg

Percentage of Recommended Daily Intake Vitamin C - 13%

Apple Preservation

Prevent Discoloration

The addition of Ascorbic acid (Vitamin C) to light coloured fruits at the time of canning will help prevent discoloration. Tablet or crystalline form may be used. Put 5 tablets of 50 milligrams in bottom of each quart jar before packing fruit; or add 1/2 teaspoon of crystalline Ascorbic acid to each quart of the syrup before pouring over fruit in jars, or use commercial Ascorbic and Citric acid mixture following manufacturer's directions.

Using Apples in Canning

Apples are a welcome fruit to the enthusiastic canner. Alone or as a compliment or base to other fruits, the apple regales us with its versatility. The natural acids in fruit make them ideal for canning while many vegetables have a very low acid content. The addition of vinegars, lemon juices and other acids to the pickling of vegetables make them a less risky prospect. The combinations of fruits for jellies, jams and preserves are unlimited but it is amazing to see how often apples are a part of these combinations. A heat processing should always be a part of your canning regime, as it produces an airless vacuum seal and destroys the enzymes and microorganisms that spoils the fruit and its flavour. This is an all day project and requires a fair amount of concentration and timing.

Select uniform apples. Wash, pare and core. Cut into desired size. If peeled fruit is to stand several minutes before precooking, drop it into solution to prevent discoloration. Drain. Boil 3 to 5 minutes in a thin syrup (see below). Pack into jars to within 1/2 inch of top. Fill to within 1/2 inch of top of jar with boiling syrup. Put on cap, screw band firmly tight. Process in boiling water bath as follows: 20 minutes - pint jars 25 minutes - quart jars

Drying Apples

The process of drying fruit is a way to preserve the extra fruit left over after canning is complete. One of the oldest methods of preserving fruit, it is based on the premise that bacteria thrive in a moist environment. Drying the fruit eliminates the moisture and thereby eliminates the action of the bacteria that is responsible for spoiling fruit. Apples are among the most popular fruit to dry because they stand up to the drying process and are most useful as a dried fruit.

First clean, wash and trim the apples. To dry the fruit out entirely you need a steady source of heat, the sun is best, but can be unreliable. A moderate breeze or a draft is also helpful. Fruit can be dried in short bursts, as the sugar inhibits moulds. Whatever method you choose, when the fruit is dry leave it at room temperature overnight to 'condition' then store it.

Preparing the Apples for Drying

Use ripe, cooking or eating apples. Peel, core and slice into 1/4 inch thick rings, dropping the rings into a lightly salted water bath (2 tablespoons per gallon) to prevent browning. An alternative is to use 1 teaspoon of ascorbic acid per 2 ½ cups of water. The darkening of dried fruit doesn't affect the flavour, but some people find the end product is not attractive.

Oven Method

Shake off the water and thread on sticks or spread on trays. The sticks can then be propped up above the stove, or supported on trays in the oven. The oven heat should be no more than 140 degrees. An oven thermometer might come in handy to regulate the temperature precisely. If heat is continuous, the rings take 4-6 hours to dry; if intermittent, 2 to 3 days. They are ready when their texture is like a chamois.

Sun Method

Using the natural heat of the sun is the most inexpensive and produces the best flavour. If you chose to use the sun's heat to dry your apples you will need a large lightweight tray on which to spread the apples. Since you will want the air to circulate freely under and around the apples, wooden frames with wire or cheesecloth stapled on are a handy solution. To protect from insects you should cover the trays with a cheesecloth. The inconvenience is if it rains the whole thing must be brought inside. Using a cold frame is another way to dry apples outdoors.

Storing Dried Apples

Any dried fruit or vegetable must be protected so that the moisture in the air is not re absorbed into the food. Airtight glass jars or zip-locked plastic bags, with the air squeezed out, are fine. They can also be packaged and frozen. Keep moisture away from the dried apple until ready to use.

Freezing

Peel, core, and slice apples. Put in solution to prevent darkening. Drain and blanch 2 minutes in boiling water or slice directly into chilled syrup (see below) in bags or empty, cleaned milk cartons, then freeze.

Syrup
1 cup sugar
3 cups water
Boil sugar and water together until sugar is dissolved.

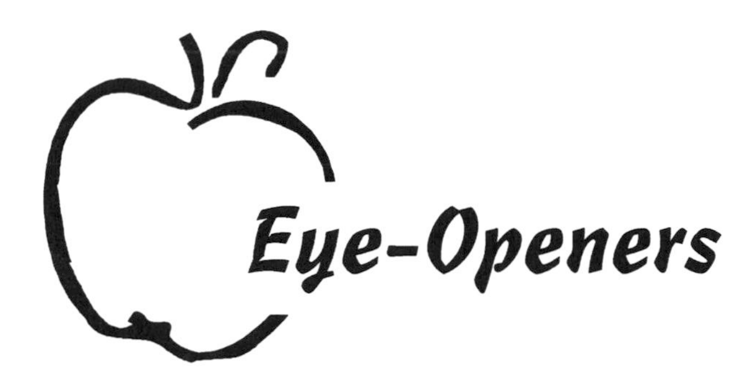

Eye-Openers

When making pancakes or oatmeal, choose from:

Cortland
Idared
McIntosh
Golden Delicious
Spartan
Crispin (Mutsu)
Empire

Nasturtium, Apple and Almond Pancake

Jacqueline Tames proudly claims she lives in the "finest Apple producing area in Canada". As an accomplished gardener, she cheerfully brings flowers to the kitchen, and this recipe to us.

1/4 cup	**sparkling mineral water**	***50 mL***
1 cup	**milk**	***250 mL***
1 cup	**nasturtium petals**	***250 mL***
1-1/2 cups	**all-purpose flour**	***375 mL***
1/2 cup	**almonds, chopped**	***125 mL***
3/4 cup	**Apples, diced, peeled and cored**	***175 mL***
3 tbsp	**vanilla extract**	***45 mL***
2 tbsp	**baking powder**	***25 mL***
3 tbsp	**sugar**	***45 mL***
3	**eggs**	***3***
4 tbsp	**canola oil**	***60 mL***
1 tbsp	**butter**	***15 mL***

Combine mineral water and milk together. With care, incorporate the rest of the ingredients except 1 tbsp butter without overmixing. Try to make it as smooth as possible. In an electric frying pan, melt 1 tbsp butter; when it foams, add enough batter to make desired size pancakes. Cook for 2 or 3 minutes or until lightly browned, then turn over and finish the other side. Drizzle with syrup and serve.

Makes 4 to 6 servings.

Old-Fashioned Oatmeal with Apples, Raisins and Honey-Toasted Walnuts

This homey, comforting cereal is like warm granola, especially with the crunchy honey-toasted walnut topping.

1/4 cup	**coarsely chopped walnuts**	*50 mL*
1 tbsp	**honey**	*15 mL*
3 cups	**water**	*750 mL*
2 cups	**old-fashioned oats**	*500 mL*
1 tsp	**salt**	*5 mL*
1 cup	**pure Apple juice**	*250 mL*
1 cup	**Apple finely chopped peeled**	*250 mL*
1/4 cup	**(packed) golden brown sugar**	*50 mL*
1/4 cup	**raisins**	*50 mL*
1/2 tsp	**ground cinnamon**	*2 mL*
1/2 cup	**plain yogurt**	*125 mL*

Stir chopped walnuts in small nonstick saucepan over medium heat until lightly toasted, about 3 minutes. Drizzle with honey stirring until honey thickens and coats nuts, about 2 minutes. Remove saucepan from heat. Stir to loosen nuts from saucepan and cool.

Bring 3 cups water to boil in heavy medium saucepan. Add oats and salt and stir over medium heat until oats are softened and very thick, about 5 minutes. Stir in Apple juice, chopped Apple, brown sugar, raisins and cinnamon. Reduce heat to low, cover and cook until Apples are tender, about 5 minutes.

Divide cereal among 4 bowls. Top with yogurt and honey-toasted walnuts.

Makes 4 servings.

Baked Pancake With Apple-Raspberry Compote

Really an overgrown popover, this baked pancake makes an easy, delicious breakfast for company.

Apple-Raspberry Compote:

2 tsp	**butter**	***10 mL***
4	**Apples, peeled, cored and thinly sliced**	***4***
1/2 cup	**sugar**	***125 mL***
1/4 cup	**Apple cider or pure Apple juice**	***50 mL***
2 tbsp	**fresh lemon juice**	***25 mL***
1 cup	**fresh raspberries**	***250 mL***

Pancake:

3	**large eggs**	***3***
2	**large egg whites**	***2***
1/2 cup	**all-purpose white flour**	***125 mL***
2 tbsp	**sugar**	***25 mL***
1/4 tsp	**salt**	***1 mL***
1 cup	**milk**	***250 mL***
2 tsp	**pure vanilla extract**	***10 mL***
	confectioners' sugar for dusting	

To make Apple-raspberry compote:

In a large nonstick saucepan, melt butter over medium heat. Add Apples and sauté for 2 minutes. Stir in sugar, Apple cider or juice and lemon juice. Reduce heat to low and simmer, stirring occasionally, until the Apples are tender but still hold their shape, 5 to 7 minutes. (The compote can be prepared ahead to this point and stored, covered, in the refrigerator for up to 2 days. Warm gently before continuing.) Stir in raspberries.

To make pancake:
Preheat oven to 425 degrees F. Place an ovenproof 10-inch nonstick saucepan in the oven to heat for 10 to 15 minutes.

In a large bowl, whisk eggs and egg whites. Add flour, sugar and salt and whisk until smooth. Gradually whisk in milk and vanilla. Pour into the hot saucepan and bake for 15 to 20 minutes, or until the pancake is puffed and golden. Loosen edges and slide the pancake onto a serving platter. Dust with confectioners' sugar and serve with Apple-raspberry compote.

Notes:

PRINCE EDWARD COUNTY
Commercial
Feature
JUICY SWEET
FLAV-R-FUL
NATUR-ALLY GOOD
Be satisfied with nothing less
So crisp you can hear the taste.
They taste as good as they sound.

When making soups, sauces or purées, choose from:

Cortland
Empire
Northern Spy
McIntosh
Golden Delicious

Apple Soup

Not only is soup a great meal in itself, but when served as a first course, it may help you lose weight. Of course we recommend you use the nonfat sour cream.

16	**Apples, cored and chopped**	***16***
5 cups	**water**	***1.25L***
1/2 tbsp	**lemon peel, grated**	***7.5 mL***
1 inch	**cinnamon stick**	***2.5 cm***
1/4 cup	**maple syrup**	***50 mL***
1 tbsp	**arrowroot**	***15 mL***
1 tbsp	**lemon juice**	***15 mL***
1/4 cup	**white wine**	***50 mL***
1/2 cup	**sour cream**	***125 mL***

Simmer Apples, water, lemon peel, cinnamon, and maple syrup until Apples are tender, about 20 minutes; remove cinnamon. Purée soup in blender; return to saucepan. Remove about a cup of liquid and combine it with arrowroot. When thickened, return to soup. Stir in lemon juice, and wine. Heat through. Garnish each bowl with a spoonful of sour cream.

Makes 6 servings.

Apple Fennel Soup

When the impulse strikes, here's a flavourful puréed soup that can be prepared in just 30 minutes. Macintosh Apples are quite suitable, but Idared, Cortland and Spys shouldn't be discounted!

1 1/2 cups	**chicken broth**	***375 mL***
2 cups	**water**	***500 mL***
1/2 cup	**white wine**	***125 mL***
2	**Apples, peeled, cored, and chopped**	***2***
1 cup	**thinly sliced carrots**	***250 mL***
1	**small onion, thinly sliced**	***1***
1/2 cup	**chopped fresh fennel**	***125 mL***
1	**bay leaf**	***1***
1/4 tsp	**dried thyme leaves**	***1 mL***
6	**black peppercorns**	***6***
	plain yogurt	

[illegible]rge pot, combine broth, water, wine, Apples, carrots, onion, [illegible], bay leaf, thyme, and peppercorns; heat to boiling. Reduce [illegible]o simmer, cover, and cook 20 minutes.

[illegible]ain soup, reserving liquid. Remove bay leaf from Apple-[illegible]egetable mixture. In blender or food processor, purée mixture; add reserved liquid and blend well. Reheat soup if necessary. To serve, ladle into soup bowls and top with dollop of yogurt, if desired.

Makes 4 servings.

Butternut Squash and Apple Soup

This tasty treat is a winter delight.

3 tbsp	**canola oil**	***45 mL***
1 lb	**butternut squash, peeled and chopped**	***500 g***
1 lb	**Apples, peeled, cored, and quartered**	***500 g***
1/2 lb	**onions, sliced**	***250 g***
3	**slices white bread, cubed**	***3***
6 cups	**chicken stock**	***1.5 L***
1/4 tsp	**dried tarragon, crumbled**	***1 mL***
	salt and freshly ground white pepper	
1 cup	**half & half**	***250 mL***
1/3 cup	**dry Sherry or dry vermouth**	***75mL***
	sour cream	
	snipped fresh chives	

Heat oil in heavy large pot over low heat. Add squash, Apples, onions and bread and sauté 5 minutes. Add stock, tarragon, salt and pepper and bring to a boil. Reduce heat to low. Cover and simmer until squash and Apples are very tender, about 50 minutes.

Cool soup slightly. Purée in batches in processor. (Can be prepared 1 day ahead. Cool, cover, & refrigerate.) Add cream and sherry to soup and bring to simmer. Season. Ladle soup into bowls and top each with a dollop of sour cream. Sprinkle with chives.

Makes 8 servings.

Curried Cauliflower Apple Soup

This delicious soup can be prepared in 45 minutes or less. Substitute buttermilk instead of the cream if you are watching your weight!

1	**small onion, chopped fine**	***1***
1	**small garlic clove, minced**	***1***
1/2 tsp	**curry powder**	***2 mL***
1 1/2 tbsp	**unsalted butter**	***22 mL***
1	**Apple**	***1***
4 cups	**cauliflower flowerets**	***1L***
1 1/2 cups	**chicken broth**	***375 mL***
1 cup	**water**	***250 mL***
1/4 cup	**heavy cream**	***50 ml***
	salt & pepper to taste	

In a 3 1/2- to 4-quart saucepan cook onion, garlic, and curry powder in butter over moderately low heat, stirring, until onion is softened. Peel and core Apple. Chop Apple coarsely and add to curry mixture. Add cauliflower, broth, and water and simmer, covered, until cauliflower is very tender, 15 to 20 minutes.

In a blender or food processor purée soup in batches until very smooth, transferring as puréed to another saucepan. Stir in cream and salt and pepper to taste and heat over moderate heat until hot.

Makes about 4 cups

Apple-Cheese Soup

Cold weather soup, diced Apples and cheese make it colourful. Easily made without the ham or bacon. Use vegetable broth instead of the chicken stock.

	***bouquet garni:**	
1 tbsp	**white peppercorns**	*15 mL*
3	**sprigs fresh thyme**	*3*
2	**bay leaves (tied together in cheesecloth)**	*2*
1/4 cup	**canola oil**	*50 mL*
3 oz	**ham scraps and/or 1 ham bone**	*75 g*
1	**stalk celery diced**	*1*
2	**cloves garlic minced**	*2*
2	**onions diced**	*2*
8	**Apples peeled, cored and quartered**	*8*
1 cup	**white port**	*250 mL*
6 cups	**chicken broth**	*1.5 L*
4	**slices bacon for garnish**	*4*
1	**McIntosh Apple for garnish**	*1*
1	**Golden Delicious Apple for garnish**	*1*
	juice of 1 lemon	
1/4 cup	**unsalted butter softened**	*50 mL*
1/4 cup	**all-purpose flour**	*50 mL*
1 1/2 lbs	**old Cheddar cheese grated**	*750 g*
	salt and/or hot sauce to taste	

In a medium-size saucepan heat the oil over medium-high heat. Add the ham scraps, celery, garlic, and onions and sauté for about 4 minutes, or until the onions are tender.

Reduce the heat to medium and add the quartered Apples. Cover and cook, stirring frequently, for about 10 minutes or until the Apples soften. Add the port and simmer for 5 minutes more. Add the chicken stock, bouquet garni, and ham bone, if using. Reduce the heat to low and simmer, partially covered, for about 20 minutes, or until the flavours are well blended. Remove the bouquet garni. (The soup may be made a day or two in advance, up to this point. Cool and refrigerate.)

Meanwhile in a small saucepan, fry the bacon over medium heat for about 5 minutes, or until browned and crisp. Drain on paper towels. Cut into 1 inch dice and set aside.

Leaving the skin on, cut the Golden Delicious and McIntosh Apples into 1/8-inch dice to use for garnish – 2 tbsp of each colour. Put the diced Apples in a small glass or ceramic bowl and sprinkle with 1 tbsp of the lemon juice. Set aside.

In a small bowl, knead the softened butter and flour together until smooth to make a 'beurre manie'. Whisk the mixture into the soup to thicken it. Cook for 5 minutes longer, stirring frequently. Add the grated cheese to the soup, stirring constantly, until it is melted.

Strain the soup through a fine sieve into the top of doubleboiler set over gently boiling water to keep the soup hot. (Do not press too hard on the solids.) Season with the remaining lemon juice, add salt and hot sauce to taste. Ladle the soup into warm serving bowls and garnish with the diced Apples and chopped bacon. Serve hot.

Makes 6 servings.

Curried Butternut Squash Bisque

A velvety, spicy first-course soup.

2 tsp	**canola oil**	***10 mL***
2	**onions, chopped**	***2***
3	**cloves garlic, minced**	***3***
1 tbsp	**curry powder**	***15 mL***
1/2 tsp	**ground cumin**	***2 mL***
6 cups	**chicken stock**	***1.5 L***
1 cup	**Apple cider**	***250 mL***
1/2 cup	**white rice**	***125 mL***
2 lbs	**butternut squash, peeled and cubed**	***1 kg***
	salt & freshly ground black pepper	
1/2 cup	**plain yogurt**	***125 mL***
2 tbsp	**milk**	***25 mL***

In a heavy soup pot, heat oil over medium heat. Add onions and garlic; sauté for 2 to 3 minutes, or until softened. Stir in curry and cumin and cook for 1 minute. Add chicken stock, cider, rice and squash; bring to a boil. Reduce heat to low and cover the pan; simmer for 30 to 40 minutes, or until the squash is tender. Strain the mixture and purée the solids in a food processor or blender until very smooth. Return the purée and liquid to the saucepan.

To serve, heat the soup gently and season with salt and pepper. In a small bowl, stir together yogurt and milk. Ladle the soup into bowls, and add a dollop of the yogurt mixture. Draw the tip of a knife or a toothpick through the yogurt to make decorative swirls.

Makes 6 servings

Breads & Appetizers

When a sauce texture is required, choose from:

Cortland
Empire
McIntosh
Golden Delicious
Russet
Northern Spy

When a firmer, 'pie' texture is required, choose from:

Cortland
Spartan
Idared
Crispin (Mutsu)
McIntosh
Russet
Northern Spy
Golden Delicious

Apple Butter Bread

You will find the Apple butter recipe on page 100.

2 cups	**all-purpose flour**	***500 mL***
1 cup	**brown sugar**	***250 mL***
1 1/2 tsp	**baking powder**	***7 mL***
1/2 tsp	**baking soda**	***2 mL***
1/2 tsp	**salt**	***2 mL***
1 1/2 cup	**Apple butter, divided use**	***375 mL***
1/2 cup	**Apple juice**	***125 mL***
1/4 cup	**butter, melted**	***50 mL***
1	**egg, beaten**	***1***
1 cup	**raisins (optional)**	***250 mL***
1/2 cup	**chopped walnuts**	***125 mL***

Preheat oven to 350 degrees F. Grease and flour bottom and sides of a 9 x 5 x 3" loaf pan; set aside.

Combine flour, brown sugar, baking powder, soda and salt in a large bowl. Stir in 3/4 cup Apple butter, Apple juice, butter and egg. Fold in raisins and walnuts. Pour half of the batter into prepared pan. Spread remaining 3/4 cup Apple butter over batter. Gently pour remaining batter over Apple butter.

Bake 60-75 minutes or until top springs back when lightly touched in centre. Set pan on a wire rack to cool for 15 minutes, then remove bread from pan and continue cooling on rack. Wrap bread tightly with plastic wrap and store in refrigerator.

Makes 1 loaf.

Baked Brie with Fresh Cranberries and Apples

The aroma of brie baking with Apples and cranberries is mouth-watering!

1	**four-inch round brie cheese**	*1*
1 cup	**fresh cranberries**	*250 mL*
1	**Apple cored and diced**	*1*
1 cup	**cranberry/Apple juice**	*250 mL*

Preheat oven to 350 degrees F. Put cranberries, Apple and juice in a saucepan and boil gently for 3 minutes. Place brie in a round ovenproof dish, slightly larger than the brie.

Strain the liquid from the cranberry/Apple mixture and put the mixture on top of the brie. Bake for 15 to 20 minutes. Serve with sliced French bread.

Notes:

Apple, Goat Cheese & Prosciutto Bruschetta

Linda Reidt of Zephyr Farms in Baltimore, Ontario, raises her own goats and uses their milk to make her own cheeses. She says that because so many of our Apple varieties store so well, this Italian-style appetizer is a year-round favorite at her house.

1/4 cup	**goat cheese, softened**	*50mL*
3/4 tsp	**minced fresh thyme leaves, or 1/4 teaspoon dried thyme**	*3 mL*
1/4 tsp	**ground black pepper**	*1 mL*
8	**slices crusty bread**	*8*
8	**thin slices prosciutto**	*8*
1	**Apple, cored and very thinly sliced**	*1*

Preheat broiler. Combine cheese, thyme and black pepper; set aside. Place bread on baking sheet; broil, about 6 inches from heat, until lightly toasted. Loosely pleat prosciutto onto bread. Cut each piece of bread in half and arrange Apple slices, then cheese mixture, over prosciutto.

Place bruschetta on baking sheet. Broil until cheese softens slightly. Serve as a first course or pass as an hors d'oeuvre.

Makes 8 servings.

Cider Welsh Rarebit

Delicious. This one is from Grant Howes, of The County Cider Company, Prince Edward County.

1 litre	**Apple cider**	***1 L***
1 tbsp	**Dijon mustard**	***15 mL***
1 tbsp	**worcestershire sauce**	***15 mL***
1 1/2 lb	**old cheddar cheese, grated**	***750 g***
	thinly sliced baguette - toasted	

Pour Apple cider into a large pot on high heat, reduce to 1/6th. Turn down heat to medium. Add mustard and worcestershire sauce and slowly add grated cheese constantly stirring until a nice thick, smooth consistency is achieved. Be careful not to boil.

Remove from heat. Spread on toasted baguette and glaze under the broiler. Serve hot. Extra rarebit keeps well in the refrigerator.

Notes:

Apple Cheddar Scones

Unlike traditional scone recipes that call for generous amounts of butter and cream, this version is leaner and lighter, though rich in Apple flavor.

1 1/2 cups	**all-purpose flour**	***375 mL***
1/2 cup	**toasted wheat germ**	***125 mL***
3 tbsp	**sugar**	***45 mL***
2 tsp	**baking powder**	***10 mL***
1/2 tsp	**salt**	***2 mL***
2 tbsp	**butter**	***25 mL***
1	**Apple, cored and finely chopped**	***1***
1/4 cup	**shredded cheddar cheese**	***50 mL***
1	**large egg white**	***1***
1/2 cup	**milk**	***125 mL***

Heat oven to 400 degrees F. Grease an 8-inch round cake pan. In medium bowl, combine flour, wheat germ, sugar, baking powder, and salt. With pastry blender or fork, cut in butter until mixture is crumbly.

Stir in Apple and cheddar cheese. Beat egg white and milk together. Add to flour mixture, mixing gently, until soft dough forms. Turn dough out onto lightly floured surface and knead 4 times.

Spread dough evenly in cake pan and score deeply with knife to make six wedges. Bake 25 to 30 minutes or until top springs back when gently pressed. Cool until warm or room temperature.

Makes 6 scones.

Apple Cheese Quick Bread

1/2 cup	**unsalted butter, softened**	*125 mL*
1/3 cup	**sugar**	*75 mL*
1/3 cup	**honey**	*75 mL*
2	**large eggs**	*2*
1 cup	**whole-wheat flour**	*250 mL*
1 cup	**all-purpose flour**	*250 mL*
1 tsp	**double-acting baking powder**	*5 mL*
1/2 tsp	**baking soda**	*2 mL*
1/2 tsp	**salt**	*2 mL*
1 1/2 cups	**Apples, peeled, cored and chopped**	*375 mL*
1/2 cup	**grated Swiss cheese**	*125 mL*
1/2 cup	**chopped walnuts**	*125 mL*
	cream cheese as an accompaniment	

In a large bowl cream together the butter and sugar, beat in the honey and eggs. Into the butter mixture sift together the flours, baking powder, baking soda, and salt; stir the mixture until it is combined well, and fold in the Apples, cheese, and walnuts.

Spoon batter into a buttered loaf pan, 9 x 5 x 3", and bake in the middle of a preheated 350 degree F oven for 50 to 60 minutes, or until it makes a hollow sound when tapped. Turn the bread out onto a rack, and let it cool completely. Serve it sliced with cream cheese.

Makes 1 loaf.

Apple and Onion Tart

When we see garlic in a recipe we usually double the amount; we tried that with this one and found it overpowered the Apple/onion flavours.

1 package	**active dry yeast**	***1***
1 tbsp	**plus 1 teaspoon sugar**	***15 mL***
1 cup	**warm water**	***250 mL***
1/2 cup	**rye flour**	***125 mL***
2 tbsp	**olive oil**	***25 mL***
1 tsp	**salt**	***5 mL***
2 cup	**all-purpose flour**	***500 mL***
2 tbsp	**olive oil**	***25 mL***
8 tbsp	**unsalted butter**	***200 mL***
7	**Apples**	***7***
1	**head of garlic**	***1***
1	**very large red onion**	***1***
1 tbsp	**ground coriander**	***15 mL***

Combine the yeast and 1 tsp sugar in a large bowl. Stir in the water and let stand 5 minutes. Whisk in the rye flour, cover the bowl, and let stand in a warm place for 20 to 30 minutes. Stir in the olive oil, salt, and all-purpose flour. Knead until smooth and elastic (about 7 to 10 minutes by hand). Place the dough in an oiled medium-size bowl and turn to coat the dough with oil. Cover and let rise in a warm place until doubled in bulk, about 1 hour.

While the dough is rising, make the Apple-garlic purée. Heat 6 tbsp of the butter in a medium-size saucepan. Add 5 Apples, peeled and cored and the peeled garlic. Simmer uncovered over low heat, stirring occasionally, until both the Apples and garlic are very soft and falling apart, about 1 hour.

Let cool slightly; then purée in a food processor. Preheat oven to 375 degrees F.

Punch the dough down and roll into a rectangle 15 x 9" on a lightly floured surface. Place on a baking sheet of the same size and crimp the edges decoratively with your fingers.

Spread the Apple-garlic purée evenly over the dough. Peel and slice the remaining 2 Apples and the onion. Arrange the sliced Apples and onions in alternating lengthwise rows over the purée. Sprinkle the top with the tbsp of sugar and the coriander. Dot the remaining 2 tbsp butter evenly over the top.

Bake the tart until the crust is light brown and the Apples are soft, about 45 minutes. Then broil the tart 6 inches from the heat to glaze the top. Serve warm.

Makes 12 servings.

Notes:

Refrigerator Apple Muffins

You can store this batter in your refrigerator for up to 3 days.

1 cup	**quick-cooking cereal**	***250 mL***
3/4 cup	**whole wheat flour**	***175 mL***
3/4 cup	**packed brown sugar**	***175 mL***
1/2 cup	**white flour**	***125 mL***
1/8 cup	**toasted wheat germ**	***30 mL***
1 tbsp	**baking powder**	***15 mL***
1 tbsp	**mixture cinnamon, nutmeg**	***15 mL***
1/2 tsp	**baking soda**	***2 mL***
1/2 tsp	**salt**	***2 mL***
1 cup	**Apple, chopped peeled**	***250 mL***
2	**lightly beaten eggs**	***2***
1 1/4 cup	**skim milk**	***310 mL***
1/3 cup	**cooking oil**	***75 mL***
	sugar	

In a large mixing bowl stir together cereal, whole-wheat flour, brown sugar, white flour, wheat germ, baking powder, cinnamon and nutmeg, baking soda, and salt. Add the chopped Apples; stir to coat with flour mixture. In a small mixing bowl combine eggs, milk, and oil. Add to the flour mixture; stir until just moistened.

Line muffin pan with paper baking cups. Spoon the batter into the cups, filling cups two-thirds full. Sprinkle muffin tops with some of the sugar. Bake in a preheated 400 degree F oven for 18 to 20 minutes, or till golden brown. Remove from pans; cool slightly on racks.

Makes 18 muffins.

Apple Oat Bran Muffins

Low in cholesterol and saturated fat, these scrumptious homemade muffins are much healthier than the average store-bought variety.

3/4 cup	**all-purpose flour**	***175 mL***
3/4 cup	**whole wheat flour**	***175 mL***
1 1/2 tsp	**cinnamon**	***7 mL***
1 tsp	**baking powder**	***5 mL***
1/2 tsp	**baking soda**	***2 mL***
1/4 tsp	**salt**	***1 mL***
1 cup	**buttermilk**	***500 mL***
1/2 cup	**oat bran**	***125 mL***
1/4 cup	**firmly packed brown sugar**	***50 mL***
2 tbsp	**vegetable oil**	***25 mL***
1	**large egg**	***1***
1 1/2 cups	**Apples peeled, cored, chopped**	***375 mL***

Heat oven to 400 degrees F. Line muffin tins with paper liners. In large bowl, combine both flours, cinnamon, baking powder, baking soda, and salt. In medium bowl, beat buttermilk, oat bran, brown sugar, oil, and egg until blended.

Stir buttermilk mixture into flour mixture until just combined. Fold in Apples. Divide batter among muffin cups. Bake 18 to 20 minutes or until wooden pick inserted in centers comes out clean. Cool muffins in pan 5 minutes; remove from pan and cool on wire rack.

Makes 12 muffins

Apple Almond Bread

1 cup	**flour, all-purpose**	***250 mL***
1/2 cup	**whole wheat flour**	***125 mL***
1 tsp	**baking powder**	***5 mL***
1/2 tsp	**baking soda**	***2 mL***
1/2 tsp	**cinnamon**	***2 mL***
1/4 tsp	**nutmeg**	***1 mL***
1/4 cup	**margarine**	***50 mL***
1/2 cup	**sugar**	***125 mL***
3	**egg whites**	***3***
1 tsp	**almond flavouring**	***5 mL***
1/2 cup	**buttermilk**	***125 mL***
2 cup	**Apples, chopped, peeled**	***500 mL***
	nonstick vegetable oil spray	

Stir together flours, baking powder, soda, cinnamon and nutmeg; set aside.

In large bowl with an electric mixer on medium speed, beat together margarine and sugar until combined. Mix in egg whites and almond flavouring. Add flour mixture and buttermilk alternately, mixing thoroughly after each addition. Fold in Apples. Spread evenly in spray-coated 9 x 5 x 3" loaf pan.

Bake in 350 degree F oven about 50 minutes or until golden brown and wooden toothpick comes out clean. Remove from pan and cool on wire rack before cutting.

Makes 1 loaf.

Salads

When making salads, choose from:

Cortland
McIntosh
Golden Delicious
Spartan
Crispin (Mutsu)
Empire
Red Delicious

Dressings for Salads

Cider Vinaigrette

1/4 cup	vegetable oil	*50 mL*
3 tbsp	cider vinegar	*45 mL*
1 tbsp	minced onion	*15 mL*
1 tsp	Dijon mustard	*5 mL*
1/2 tsp	sugar	*2 mL*

Honey-Cream Dressing:

1/4 cup	sour cream	*50 mL*
1 cup	small-curd cottage cheese, creamed	*250 mL*
1 cup	plain yogurt	*250 mL*
2 tbsp	honey	*25 mL*
2 tsp	lime juice	*10 mL*

Cardamon Cream Dressing:

1/2 cup	plain yogurt	*125 mL*
1/2 tsp	honey	*2 mL*
1/4 tsp	ground cardamon or cinnamon	*1 mL*
1 tbsp	toasted coconut (garnish)	*15 mL*

Citrus Dressing:

1/2 cup	plain yogurt,	*125 mL*
1/4 cup	orange juice concentrate, thawed	*50 mL*
	dash nutmeg	

Yogurt Dressing:

1/2 cup	plain yogurt	*125 mL*
3 tbsp	mayonnaise	*45 mL*
3 tbsp	cider vinegar	*45 mL*
1 tbsp	sugar	*15 mL*
1/8 tsp	ground black pepper	*.5 mL*

Sherry Ambrosia

2/3 cup	**orange sections**	*150 mL*
1 cup	**fresh grapefruit sections**	*250 mL*
2	**Apples**	*2*
2 tbsp	**dry sherry**	*25 mL*
1 tsp	**fresh lemon juice**	*5 mL*
2 tsp	**sugar**	*10 mL*
1/3 cup	**sliced banana**	*75 mL*
2 tbsp	**shredded coconut**	*25 mL*
3	**maraschino cherries, drained**	*3*

Cut orange sections into halves, grapefruit sections into quarters, and cored (but not peeled) Apples into small bite-sized cubes. Mix these fruits with sherry, lemon juice, and sugar. Cover and chill for 1 hour or longer.

Just before serving, add banana; mix well. Spoon into 6 individual dessert dishes. Scatter coconut on top of fruit. Slice maraschino cherries; place a few slices on top of coconut.

Makes 3 servings.

Notes:

Apple Bean Salad

Use Red Delicious, McIntosh, Spartan or any other of your favourite salad Apples.

1 can	**(16-ounce) dark red kidney beans, rinsed and drained**	*1*
2	**Apples, cored and chopped**	*2*
1/4 cup	**finely chopped green onion**	*50 mL*
1/4 cup	**finely chopped celery**	*50 mL*
1/4 cup	**finely chopped mild green chilies**	*50 mL*
1 1/2 tbsp	**white wine vinegar**	*22 mL*
1 tbsp	**vegetable oil**	*15 mL*
1/2 tbsp	**sesame oil**	*7 mL*
1/8 tsp	**salt**	*.5 mL*
	dash hot red pepper sauce (optional)	
	toasted sesame seeds	

In medium-size bowl, combine beans, Apples, green onion, celery, and chilies; mix well. In small bowl, mix together vinegar, oils, salt and hot red pepper sauce (if desired); stir into bean mixture. Cover and refrigerate at least 30 minutes before serving. Lightly toast sesame seeds in a saucepan and use as garnish.

Makes 4 servings.

Apple Cabbage Coleslaw

Dressing:		
1/4 cup	**sugar**	*50 mL*
1 tsp	**corn starch**	*5 mL*
1/2 tsp	**celery seed**	*2 mL*
1/4 tsp	**salt**	*1 mL*
1/8 tsp	**dry mustard**	*.5 mL*
3/4 cup	**sweet cider**	*175 mL*
3 tsp	**cider vinegar**	*15 mL*
2 tbsp	**mayonnaise**	*25 mL*
2 tbsp	**plain yogurt**	*25 mL*
6 cups	**shredded cabbage**	*1.8 L*
2	**Apples cored and chopped**	*2*

Combine sugar, corn starch, celery seed, salt and dry mustard in 2-cup microwave-safe container. Gradually stir in sweet cider and vinegar until smooth. Microwave on high, uncovered, for 3 to 3 1/2 minutes or until mixture boils and thickens slightly, stirring once. Refrigerate until chilled, about 3 hours.

Mix mayonnaise together with yogurt and combine with refrigerated mixture. Combine cabbage and Apples in serving bowl and pour on dressing. Toss lightly to coat. Serve immediately or refrigerate.

Makes 4 servings.

Apple Roquefort Salad

This is a very nice salad providing a great combination of flavours and textures. The key is to make sure all ingredients are really fresh and that the apples are crisp. Red Delicious are the best.

	Cider Vinaigrette (page 48)	
3	**Apples, unpeeled, quartered lengthwise and cored**	*3*
1/3 cup	**crumbled Roquefort cheese**	*75 mL*
3 tbsp	**coarsely chopped walnuts**	*45 mL*
1	**small Belgian Endive, trimmed and rinsed**	*1*
1	**bunch watercress, rinsed, dried, stems removed**	*1*
	salt	
	freshly ground black pepper	

Make Cider Vinaigrette. Slice each unpeeled Apple quarter lengthwise into 8 thin slices and toss with the Roquefort, walnuts and 3 tbsp of the dressing in a medium bowl. Refrigerate, covered, for about 3 hours, tossing occasionally.

At serving time, cut the endive crosswise into thirds and combine with the watercress and Apple mixture in a serving bowl. Whisk remaining dressing briefly and add 2 - 3 tbsp to the salad and toss well. Taste and adjust seasoning with salt and pepper if desired. Toss again and serve immediately.

Apple Beet Salad

Crunchy, bright, and tangy, this salad stands up well to hearty meats or poultry dishes.

4	**Apples, peeled, cored, and sliced**	*4*
1 can (16-oz)	**julienne beets, drained**	*1*
1/2 cup	**sliced radishes**	*125 mL*
1/4 cup	**diagonally sliced green onions**	*50 mL*
1/4 cup	**vinegar**	*50 mL*
1/4 cup	**olive oil**	*50 mL*
1 tsp	**sugar**	*5 mL*
1/4 tsp	**ground allspice**	*1 mL*
	salt and pepper to taste	
	dash hot sauce (optional)	

In large bowl, combine Apples, beets, radishes, and green onions. In small bowl, vinegar, olive oil, sugar, allspice, salt, pepper, and, if desired, hot sauce; pour over Apple mixture and toss well. Cover and refrigerate at least 1 hour before serving.

Makes 6 servings.

Apple Cabbage Kiwi Salad

1/3 cup	**honey**	***75 mL***
1/4 cup	**lime juice**	***50 mL***
1/2 tsp	**grated lime zest**	***2 mL***
1/2 tsp	**dried mustard**	***2 mL***
1/8 tsp	**salt**	***.5 mL***
3	**Apples**	***3***
4 cups	**shredded cabbage**	***1 L***
2	**kiwi fruit, peeled and sliced**	***2***
2	**green onions, chopped**	***2***
	lettuce leaves	

In large bowl, whisk together honey, lime juice, lime zest, mustard, and salt to make dressing. Core one Apple and cut into thin strips; add to dressing. Add cabbage, kiwi fruit, and green onion; toss well. To serve, arrange lettuce on a flat platter. Core and slice remaining two Apples brush with lemon juice; arrange in a circle on top of lettuce. Mound cabbage mixture in center.

Makes 6 servings.

Notes:

Apple, Chicken and Blue Cheese Salad

Lean, not mean!

3	**Apples, cored and cubed**	*3*
3	**boneless skinless chicken breast halves, cooked and cubed**	*3*
1 cup	**seedless red grapes, cut in half**	*250 ml*
5 cup	**mixed salad greens**	*1.25 L*

Blue Cheese Dressing:

1/4 cup	**mayonnaise**	*50 mL*
1/4 cup	**crumbled blue cheese**	*50 mL*
1 1/2 tsp	**lemon juice**	*7 mL*

Toss together Apples, chicken, and grapes with blue cheese dressing. Divide greens between four salad plates. Place a generous cupful of Apple-chicken salad on each plate.

Makes 4 servings.

Carrot-Apple Salad

1 cup	**shredded carrot**	*250 mL*
3	**Apples, unpeeled and diced**	*3*
1 tbsp	**lemon juice**	*15 mL*
1/3 cup	**mayonnaise**	*75 mL*
	salad greens	

Combine all ingredients except salad greens. Chill thoroughly. Serve on salad greens.

Makes 6 servings.

Waldorf Salad

No respectable Apple cookbook could leave out one of the most famous salads in the world. The Waldorf salad is both easy and delicious.

1 lb	**Apples**	*500 g*
2 tbsp	**lemon juice**	*25 mL*
1/2	**head celery thinly sliced**	*1/2*
1/2 cup	**coarsely chopped walnuts**	*125 mL*
1/2 cup	**mayonnaise**	*125 mL*
1 tbsp	**Dijon mustard**	*15 mL*
1	**head lettuce**	*1*

Core and slice one Apple for garnish, peel, core and chop remaining. Dip Apple slices in lemon juice to prevent discolouring. Set aside. Lightly toast the walnuts.

Blend Dijon mustard with the mayonnaise. Add the celery and walnuts to the diced Apple and mix with mayonnaise mixture. Line a serving bowl with the lettuce. Place salad in centre and garnish with Apple slices.

Makes 6 servings.

Notes:

Crab Salad with Endive and Tomato-Cilantro Sauce

The crab salad is mounded over the ends of endive spears, use them as edible scoops for the salad.

Crab Salad

2 tbsp	**olive oil**	*25 mL*
2	**shallots, thinly sliced**	*2*
1 tsp	**minced peeled fresh ginger**	*5 mL*
1/2 cup	**chopped Apple**	*125 mL*
1/2 cup	**chopped zucchini**	*125 mL*
1/2 cup	**chopped seeded red bell pepper**	*125 mL*
1/2 cup	**chopped seeded green bell pepper**	*125 mL*
1/4 cup	**chopped carrot**	*50 mL*
1/2 lb	**crabmeat, drained well**	*250 g*
1/4 cup	**mayonnaise**	*50 mL*
2 tbsp	**chopped fresh chives**	*25 mL*
	salt & pepper to taste	

Sauce

2	**tomatoes, peeled, seeded, chopped**	*2*
1/3 cup	**chopped fresh cilantro**	*75 mL*
2 tbsp	**Sherry wine vinegar**	*25 mL*
1	**garlic clove, chopped**	*1*
	Pinch of cayenne pepper	
1/2 cup	**olive oil**	*125 mL*
2	**heads Belgian endive, trimmed, separated into spears**	*2*
	Chopped fresh chives	

For Crab Salad:
Heat oil in heavy large saucepan over medium-high heat. Add shallots and ginger and sauté until tender, about 4 minutes. Add Apple, zucchini, peppers and carrot and sauté until tender but not brown, about 5 minutes. Remove from heat. Cool to room temperature.

Mix crabmeat, mayonnaise, chopped chives and sautéed Apples and vegetables in large bowl to blend. Season to taste with salt and pepper. (Can be prepared 1 day ahead. Cover and refrigerate.)

For Sauce:
Combine tomatoes, cilantro, vinegar, garlic and cayenne in blender and purée until almost smooth. Gradually add oil and blend until sauce is thick. Transfer to medium bowl. Season to taste with salt and pepper.

Arrange endive spears on large platter, tips toward platter edge. Spoon crab salad into centre of platter. Drizzle sauce over endive. Garnish salad with chopped fresh chives and serve.

Makes 6 Servings

Notes:

Fresh Fruit Compote

3	**Apples, cored and cut into 1/2 inch pieces**	*3*
2	**pears, cored and cut into 1/2 inch pieces**	*2*
1 cup	**dark raisins (optional)**	*250 mL*
1/2 cup	**orange juice**	*125 mL*
2 tbsp	**packed brown sugar**	*25 mL*
1 tbsp	**lemon juice**	*15 mL*
2	**slices fresh ginger, about 1/2 inch thick**	*2*
1/4 tsp	**ground allspice**	*1 mL*
1/2 cup	**chopped walnuts, toasted**	*125 mL*

In a 2-quart microwave bowl, combine the Apples, pears, raisins, orange juice, sugar, lemon juice, ginger, and allspice. Cover tightly with a lid or vented plastic wrap. Microwave on high for 9 to 14 minutes, or until the fruits have softened, stirring after 5 minutes. Stir in the nuts. Re-cover and let stand for 15 minutes. Remove the ginger slices. Serve warm.

Makes 4 servings.

Notes:

Curried Chicken Salad

Chilling the poached chicken breasts in the cooking liquid ensures moist, succulent results. This salad also works as a sandwich filling with lettuce in pita pockets.

2 cups	**chicken stock**	*500 mL*
6	**boneless, skinless chicken breast halves**	*6*
1/2 cup	**mayonnaise**	*125 mL*
1/2 cup	**plain yogurt**	*125 mL*
1/2 cup	**mango chutney**	*125 mL*
2 tsp	**curry powder or to taste**	*10 mL*
1	**Apple cored and chopped**	*1*
1/4 cup	**currants or raisins (optional)**	*50 mL*

In a large shallow pan, bring chicken stock to a boil. Add chicken breasts and reduce heat to low. Simmer, partially covered, for 10 to 12 minutes, or until the chicken is no longer pink inside. Transfer chicken to a shallow dish and pour the cooking liquid over the top. Refrigerate until chilled, at least 1 hour or overnight.

Remove the chicken from the cooking liquid and dice. In a medium-sized bowl, stir together mayonnaise, yogurt, chutney and curry powder until well blended. Add the diced chicken, apples and currants or raisins, tossing until thoroughly coated.

Makes 4-6 servings.

Fresh Fruit Cocktail

2 cups	**pure Apple juice**	*500 mL*
1 tbsp	**lemon juice**	*15 mL*
1/2 tsp	**grated orange or lemon peel**	*2 mL*
2 (3-inch)	**cinnamon sticks**	*2 (7.5 cm)*
2	**Apples, cored and chopped**	*2*
1 1/2 cups	**chopped fresh pineapple**	*375 mL*
1	**orange, peeled and sectioned**	*1*
1/2 cup	**seedless grapes**	*125 mL*

In medium-size saucepan, combine Apple juice, lemon juice, orange or lemon peel, and cinnamon sticks. Bring to boil and simmer, uncovered, 10 minutes. Cool; remove cinnamon sticks. In large bowl, combine Apples, pineapple, orange, and grapes. Pour cooled syrup over fruit and chill before serving.

Makes 4 servings.

Apple, Broccoli Salad

2	**Apples**	*2*
3 cups	**fresh raw broccoli, cut up**	*750 mL*
1/4 cup	**chopped walnuts**	*60 mL*
1 tbsp	**chopped red onion**	*15 mL*
1/3 cup	**raisins (optional)**	*80 mL*
1/2 cup	**plain yogurt**	*125 mL*

Core and chop Apples. Mix all ingredients together. Serve on a bed of lettuce.

Makes 4 to 6 servings.

Endive and Gorgonzola Salad

This recipe can be prepared in 45 minutes or less.

1/4 cup	**walnuts**	***50 mL***
2 tsp	**cider vinegar**	***10 mL***
1/2 tsp	**balsamic vinegar**	***2 mL***
2 1/2 tsp	**honey**	***12 mL***
2 tbsp	**extra-virgin olive oil**	***25 mL***
	salt & pepper to taste	
3	**Belgian endives**	***3***
1	**Apple**	***1***
1/4 cup	**crumbled Gorgonzola cheese**	***50 mL***
1 tsp	**minced fresh chives**	***5 mL***

Preheat oven to 350 degrees F. In a shallow baking pan toast walnuts in middle of oven until fragrant, about 10 minutes, and cool. Chop walnuts.

In a small bowl whisk together vinegars and 1/2 tsp honey and add oil in a stream, whisking until emulsified. Season dressing with salt and pepper.

Separate 4 outer leaves from each endive and arrange 3 leaves on each of 4 plates. Cut remaining endive crosswise into 1/4-inch-thick slices and put in a large bowl. Peel Apple and cut thin slices lengthwise from 4 sides, stopping just before core. Make small stacks of slices and cut stacks into thin julienne strips.

Toss sliced endive with dressing and divide among plates, mounding on whole leaves. Top salads with Gorgonzola, walnuts, Apple, chives, and salt and pepper to taste. Drizzle remaining 2 tsp honey over salads.

Makes 4 servings.

Apple Grape Salad

1	**envelope unflavoured gelatin (1 tbsp)**	*1*
1/4 cup	**water**	*50 mL*
1 1/2 cup	**pure Apple juice**	*375 mL*
1 cup	**Apple, unpeeled, diced**	*250*
1/2 cup	**red grapes, halved seeded**	*125 mL*
1/4 cup	**chopped celery**	*50 mL*

Soften gelatin in water for 5 minutes. Heat gelatin over low heat, stirring constantly, until dissolved. Add Apple juice. Chill until mixture begins to thicken. Stir in fruit and celery. Pour into 3-cup mold. Chill until set.

Makes 4 servings.

Fall Festival Fruit Salad

	Citrus Dressing (page 48)	
1	**head Iceberg lettuce**	*1*
1	**Apple, cored and thinly sliced**	*1*
1/4 lb	**grapes**	*125 g*
1	**cantaloupe, or other melon, seeded, pared, and cut into chunks**	*1*
	Pomegranate seeds (optional)	

Prepare Citrus Dressing. Core, rinse, and thoroughly drain lettuce. Using a stainless steel knife, cut into bite-size chunks. Arrange Apple slices, grape clusters, and melon wedges on lettuce. Sprinkle pomegranate seed over top. Chill. When ready to serve, drizzle Citrus Dressing over all.

Makes 4 servings.

Red And Yellow Apple Salad

The beauty of this is to use two different coloured apples. We have recommended Spartans and Crispins, but use your imagination.

1/3 cup	**Apple cider**	*75 mL*
2 tbsp	**lemon juice**	*25 mL*
2 tbsp	**cider vinegar**	*25 mL*
1 tbsp	**vegetable oil**	*15 mL*
1 tsp	**Dijon mustard**	*5 mL*
1/4 tsp	**pepper**	*1 mL*
1/8 tsp	**salt**	*.5 mL*
1/8 tsp	**ground cinnamon**	*.5 mL*
4 cups	**loosely packed torn leaf lettuce**	*1 L*
4 cups	**loosely packed torn romaine lettuce**	*1 L*
2	**Apples unpeeled, Spartan thinly sliced**	*2*
1	**Apple unpeeled, Crispin (Mutsu), thinly sliced**	*1*
2 tbsp	**sliced almonds, toasted**	*25 mL*
	freshly ground black pepper (optional)	

Combine Apple cider, lemon juice, vinegar, vegetable oil, mustard, pepper, salt, and cinnamon in a jar. Cover tightly, and shake vigorously.

Combine lettuces, Apples, and almonds in a large bowl and toss gently. Add cider mixture, and toss gently. Sprinkle with pepper, if desired.

Makes 12 servings.

Carrot, Apple & Horseradish Salad

Can be prepared in 45 minutes or less but requires additional unattended time for the horseradish to 'mature'.

2 1/2 cups	**coarsely grated carrot**	*625 mL*
2 large	**Apples**	*2*
1/2 cup	**sour cream**	*125 mL*
2 to 3 tbsp	**finely grated peeled fresh horseradish or drained bottled horseradish**	*25-45 mL*
2 tbsp	**finely chopped fresh parsley**	*25 mL*
1 tsp	**fresh lemon juice**	*5 mL*
1 tsp	**sugar**	*5 mL*
	salt & pepper to taste	

In a bowl stir together the carrots, the Apples, peeled and coarsely grated, the sour cream, the horseradish to taste, the parsley, the lemon juice, the sugar, and salt and pepper to taste. Chill the salad, covered, for 1 hour and serve.

Makes 4 to 6 servings.

Apple Salad with Lemon-Poppy Seed Dressing

1/4 cup	**mayonnaise**	*50 mL*
2 tbsp	**thawed, frozen lemonade concentrated, undiluted**	*25 mL*
1/2 tsp	**sugar**	*2 mL*
1 tsp	**poppy seeds**	*5 mL*
2	**Apples, sliced**	*2*
1/2 cup	**blueberries**	*125 mL*
1 cup	**cantaloupe balls or chunks**	*250 mL*
	leaf, Boston or bib lettuce	

Combine mayonnaise, lemonade concentrate, sugar and poppy seeds; refrigerate. Arrange Apples and fruit on lettuce. Drizzle with lemon dressing before serving.

Makes 4 servings.

Notes:

Orange Waldorf Salad

This Orange Waldorf salad is quite good, without the marshmallows.

	grated peel of 1/2 orange	
4	**oranges, peeled, cut into bite-size pieces**	*4*
1	**Apple, unpeeled, cut into bite-size pieces**	*1*
3/4 cup	**sliced celery**	*175 mL*
1 cup	**miniature marshmallows**	*250 mL*
3 tbsp	**sour cream**	*45 mL*
3 tbsp	**mayonnaise**	*45 mL*
2 tbsp	**sliced almonds**	*25 mL*
1/8 tsp	**ground cinnamon**	*.5 mL*

In large bowl, combine all ingredients; chill. Serve on salad greens, if desired.

Makes 6 servings.

Notes:

Apple Pasta Salad

A summer favourite, pasta salad, made all the more glamorous with the fruit!

1 cup	**plain yogurt**	***250 mL***
1 cup	**unsweetened crushed pineapple, undrained**	***250 mL***
1/2 tsp	**salt, optional**	***2 mL***
1/4 tsp	**garlic powder**	***1 mL***
1/4 tsp	**dry mustard**	***1 mL***
1 tsp	**finely chopped ginger**	***5 mL***
1 tbsp	**honey**	***15 mL***
2 cups	**uncooked rotini pasta**	***500 mL***
1/2 cup	**shredded carrot**	***125 mL***
1 cup	**sliced celery**	***250 mL***
1/4 cup	**sliced green onions**	***50 mL***
1/4 cup	**raisins (optional)**	***50 mL***
3 cup	**Apples diced, unpeeled**	***750 mL***

Thoroughly combine yogurt, pineapple, salt, spices, ginger and honey; refrigerate. Cook pasta according to package directions, omitting salt. Rinse with cold water and drain thoroughly. Cool completely.

In large bowl, combine all ingredients including yogurt dressing. Chill thoroughly before serving.

Makes 8 servings.

Apple Potato Salad

Terrific served at an autumn picnic.

5	**Apples, cored and sliced**	*5*
2 lbs	**red potatoes, cut into half-moon slices**	*1 kg*
1/2 cup	**celery, diced**	*125 mL*
1 cup	**mayonnaise**	*250 mL*
1/4 cup	**rice vinegar**	*50 mL*
2 tsp	**sugar**	*10 mL*
1 cup	**Applesauce**	*250 mL*
	pinch black pepper	
	pinch salt	
1 tsp	**lemon juice**	*5 mL*
1 tsp	**thyme**	*5 mL*
1 tsp	**basil**	*5 mL*

Cook potatoes in boiling water until tender. Remove, strain and cool. Mix remaining ingredients together and add to cooled potatoes and refrigerate.

Makes 8-10 servings.

Notes:

Sweet Potato & Apple Salad

Another summer favourite, the sweet potato and fresh Apple just seem to go together naturally.

2 lbs	**sweet potatoes**	*1 kg*
1/4 cup	**white wine vinegar**	*50 mL*
2 tbsp	**water**	*25 mL*
2 tbsp	**oil**	*25 mL*
2 tsp	**lemon juice**	*10 mL*
1/2 tsp	**sugar**	*2 mL*
1/2 tsp	**salt**	*2 mL*
1/2 tsp	**pepper**	*2 mL*
2	**cloves garlic, minced**	*2*
3	**Apples, each cored and cut into wedges**	*3*
6 cups	**tightly packed fresh spinach leaves**	*1.8 L*

Microwave sweet potatoes 3-4 at a time on high for 10 minutes or until tender; let cool and peel. Cut into 48 (1/4 inch thick) slices, and arrange in a large, shallow dish, overlapping slices. Combine next 8 ingredients in a small jar; cover tightly and shake vigorously. Pour over sweet potatoes; cover and let stand 1 hour.

Drain sweet potatoes, reserving vinaigrette. Toss Apples with half of reserved vinaigrette. Arrange 6 sweet potato slices and 6 Apple wedges on each of 8 spinach lined plates; drizzle with remaining vinaigrette.

Makes 8 servings.

Apple Raspberry Salad

1 3-oz	package raspberry flavoured gelatin	*1*
1 cup	boiling water	*250 mL*
1 10-oz	package frozen raspberries or 1 cup fresh raspberries	*1*
1 1/2 cup	Apples chopped, unpeeled	*375 mL*
1 cup	Applesauce	*250 mL*
1/4 cup	broken pecan pieces	*50 mL*
1/2 cup	sliced celery	*125 mL*

In 2 quart mixing bowl, dissolve gelatin in boiling water. Add frozen raspberries and stir gently until raspberries are thawed. Stir in Apples, Applesauce, pecans and celery. Pour into serving dish. Refrigerate about 2 hours or until mixture is set. Serve as salad or as an accompaniment to beef, pork or chicken.

Makes 8 servings.

Orange Nutty Salad

2	oranges, peeled, cut up	*2*
1	Apple, unpeeled, cut up	*1*
1/2 cup	sliced celery	*125 mL*
1/4 cup	raisins (optional)	*50 mL*
2 tbsp	brown sugar	*25 mL*
	juice of 1/2 lemon	
1/4 cup	coarsely chopped walnuts (toasted)	*50 mL*

In bowl, combine all ingredients except nuts; chill. Stir in nuts just before serving.

Makes 4 servings.

Apple Brown Rice Salad

3	**Apples**	***3***
2 tbsp	**lemon juice**	***25 mL***
3 1/2 cup	**cooked quick brown rice**	***875 mL***
3	**skinless, boneless chicken breast halves, cooked and cut into chunks**	***3***
1	**medium red bell pepper, seeded, trimmed and chopped**	***1***
1/4 cup	**sliced green onions**	***50 mL***

Dijon vinaigrette:

3 tbsp	**olive oil**	***45 mL***
1/4 cup	**chopped parsley**	***50 mL***
3 tbsp	**rice vinegar**	***45 mL***
2 tsp	**Dijon-style mustard**	***10 mL***
2	**cloves garlic**	***2***
1 tsp	**sugar**	***5 mL***
1/2 tsp	**salt**	***2 mL***
	black pepper to taste	

Whisk together vinaigrette ingredients until well combined. Core Apples and cut into 1 inch chunks. Gently toss with lemon juice. Combine with remaining ingredients and chill until ready to serve.

Makes 6 servings.

Notes:

Apple, Endive and Stilton Salad

For vinaigrette

2 tbsp	**white-wine vinegar**	*25 mL*
1 tbsp	**red-wine vinegar**	*15 mL*
1/2 tsp	**Dijon mustard**	*2 mL*
1/4 tsp	**sugar**	*1 mL*
2 tbsp	**extra-virgin olive oil**	*25 mL*
1	**small shallot, minced**	*1*
1/8 tsp	**salt**	*.5 mL*
	freshly ground black pepper	

2 tbsp	**unsalted butter**	*25 mL*
1 cup	**walnuts, chopped coarse**	*250 mL*
1/2 tsp	**sugar**	*2 mL*
2	**Belgian endives**	*2*
2	**Apples**	*2*
1/2 cup	**Stilton cheese, crumbled**	*125 mL*
2 tbsp	**chopped fresh tarragon leaves**	*25 mL*
	salt & freshly ground white pepper	

Make vinaigrette:
In a small bowl whisk together vinegars, mustard, and sugar. Add oil in a stream, whisking, and whisk vinaigrette until emulsified. Stir in shallot, salt and black pepper.

In a small saucepan melt butter over moderate heat and add walnuts and sugar. Cook walnuts, stirring, until golden, about 2 minutes, and transfer to a bowl. Cut endives lengthwise into julienne strips. Halve and core Apples and cut into julienne strips.

In a large bowl combine endives, Apples, walnuts, Stilton, tarragon, and vinaigrette, tossing gently, and season with salt and white pepper.

Makes 4 to 6 servings.

Brown Bag Apple Salad

1/2 cups	**orange or grapefruit juice**	*125 mL*
1 tbsp	**honey**	*15 mL*
1 tsp	**lemon or lime juice**	*5 mL*
1	**Apple, peeled, cored and chopped**	*1*
1 cup	**seedless grapes**	*250 mL*
1 cup	**orange or grapefruit sections**	*250 mL*
1/4 cup	**chopped walnuts (toasted)**	*50 mL*

In medium-size bowl, stir together orange juice, honey and lemon juice. Add Apples, grapes, orange sections and walnuts; toss to coat with juice mixture. Refrigerate or pack into individual containers for lunches and snacks.

Makes 4 servings.

Summer Apple Compote

2	**Apples**	*2*
2 cups	**watermelon cubes**	*500 mL*
1 cup	**seedless grapes**	*250 mL*
1	**orange, peeled and sliced**	*1*
1	**banana, peeled and sliced**	*1*
2 cups	**chilled ginger ale**	*500 mL*
2 tbsp	**lime juice**	*25 mL*

Core Apples and cut into bite-size pieces. Toss with watermelon, grapes, orange and banana. Combine ginger ale and lime juice. Pour over fruits. Serve immediately.

Makes 6 servings.

Spinach & Apple Salad with Almonds

1/4 cup	**minced onion**	*50 mL*
3 tbsp	**Apple cider vinegar**	*45 mL*
3 tbsp	**white wine vinegar**	*45 mL*
2 tbsp	**sesame seeds**	*25 mL*
1/4 tsp	**paprika**	*1 mL*
3 tbsp	**sugar**	*45 mL*
1/2 cup	**olive oil**	*125 mL*
2 tbsp	**butter**	*25 mL*
3/4 cup	**blanched slivered almonds**	*175 mL*
1	**10-ounce bag spinach leaves**	*1*
2	**Apples, quartered, cored, thinly sliced**	*2*

Combine onion, cider vinegar, white wine vinegar, sesame seeds and paprika in small bowl. Mix in 2 tbsp sugar. Gradually whisk in olive oil. Season dressing to taste with salt and pepper.

Melt butter in heavy large saucepan over medium heat. Add almonds. Stir until almonds begin to colour, about 2 minutes. Sprinkle remaining 1 tbsp sugar over. Stir until sugar melts and begins to turn golden, about 2 minutes longer. Transfer almonds to bowl and cool. (Dressing and almonds can be prepared 4 hours ahead. Cover separately and let stand at room temperature.)

Combine spinach and Apples in large bowl. Toss with enough dressing to coat. Mix in almonds. Serve salad, passing any remaining dressing separately.

Makes 6 to 8 Servings

Turkey Waldorf Salad

	Yogurt Dressing (page 48)	
2 cups	**sliced celery**	*500 mL*
2 cups	**cooked small shell pasta**	*500 mL*
2 cups	**diced cooked turkey breast**	*500 mL*
2 cups	**Apples diced unpeeled**	*500 mL*
1/4 cup	**sliced green onions**	*50 mL*
1/3 cup	**chopped walnuts, toasted**	*75 mL*

Combine ingredients for yogurt dressing. In a large bowl combine celery with pasta, turkey, apple, onions and walnuts. Add Yogurt dressing; toss to coat thoroughly. To toast walnuts: Place in a small dry saucepan over low heat until golden, about 5 minutes, stirring occasionally.

Makes 4 servings.

Smoked Turkey and Blue Cheese Salad

	Cider Vinaigrette dressing (page 48)	
4 cups	**chopped red leaf lettuce,**	*1 L*
1 cup	**smoked turkey, sliced**	*250 mL*
1/2	**Apple, cored and sliced**	*1/2*
1/2 cup	**blue cheese, crumbled**	*125 mL*
3 tbsp	**pecan halves**	*45 mL*
	salt & pepper to taste	

Make cider vinaigrette dressing. Combine next 5 ingredients in large bowl. Add dressing and salt to taste. Season generously with pepper. Toss well and serve.

Makes 2 servings.

Vegetables

When cooking with Apples, choose from:
Cortland
Idared
Northern Spy
McIntosh
Golden Delicious

Sweet Potatoes and Apples with Brown Sugar

This is a good dish to serve with spicy Jamaican jerked chicken, steamed greens and thick plain yogurt.

1 1/2 lbs	**sweet potatoes**	***750 g***
3	**Apples, cored and sliced**	***3***
3/4 cups	**orange juice**	***175 mL***
3/4 tsp	**grated fresh ginger**	***175 mL***
1/2 tsp	**cinnamon**	***2 mL***
1/4 tsp	**allspice**	***1 mL***
1/4 tsp	**nutmeg**	***1 mL***
2 tbsp	**brown sugar**	***25 mL***
1/2 cups	**nuts, chopped**	***125 mL***

Boil unpeeled potatoes in water for 25 minutes. Drain and cool slightly. In a medium saucepan, over high heat, heat Apples and orange juice with ginger, cinnamon, allspice, and nutmeg. Cover and cook until Apples soften, 3-5 minutes. Uncover and reduce heat; simmer Apples a few minutes longer.

While Apples are cooking, peel and slice cooked sweet potatoes. Place in casserole dish, alternating Apples and sliced sweet potatoes. Sprinkle with brown sugar and nuts and heat in microwave 4 to 5 minutes.

Makes 6 servings.

Acorn Squash and Apple Purée

The microwave techniques used here can be used in many recipes calling for cooked squash and turnips.

1	**acorn squash, halved and cleaned**	*1*
1	**Apple, cut into 1-inch pieces**	*1*
1/2 tbsp	**butter**	*7 mL*
	freshly grated nutmeg to taste if desired	
	salt & pepper to taste	

Arrange the squash, cut sides down, in a glass dish, prick the skin all over with the tip of a sharp knife, and microwave the squash at high power (100%) for 10 minutes or until tender. Put the Apple in a 1 - or 2 cup glass measuring cup, cover it with microwave-safe plastic wrap, and microwave it at high power (100%) for 4 to 6 minutes, or until it is tender.

Scoop out the squash, discarding skin, drain liquid from the Apple, and force the squash and the Apple through the medium disk of a food mill into a bowl. Reheat before serving. Stir in the butter, the nutmeg, and salt and pepper to taste.

Makes 2 servings.

Notes:

Sauerkraut with Apple and Caraway

Real country-style food, great with roast pork.

2	**jars of sauerkraut, rinsed and drained well**	*2*
2	**Apples**	*2*
3/4 cup	**dry white wine**	*175 mL*
1 cup	**chicken broth**	*250 mL*
3 tbsp	**firmly packed brown sugar**	*45 mL*
3/4 tsp	**caraway seeds**	*3 mL*

In a large heavy saucepan combine the sauerkraut, Apples, peeled and chopped, wine, broth, brown sugar, and caraway seeds and simmer the mixture, covered, stirring occasionally, for 1 hour. This can be prepared 1 day in advance, kept covered and chilled, and reheated.

Makes 8 servings.

Notes:

Apple Barley Pilaf

If you have leftovers, serve cold with a little rice vinegar and hot pepper sauce.

2 tbsp	**margarine**	*25 mL*
1/4 cup	**finely chopped onion**	*50 mL*
1/2 cup	**uncooked barley**	*125 mL*
1 cup	**chicken broth**	*250 mL*
1/4 cup	**golden raisins (optional)**	*50 mL*
1/4 tsp	**dried thyme**	*1 mL*
2	**Apples, cored and finely chopped**	*2*
2 tbsp	**chopped fresh parsley**	*25 mL*

In large saucepan with tight-fitting lid, melt margarine over medium heat. Add onion and barley; cook, stirring until golden. Add broth, raisins and thyme to barley mixture. Heat to boil; reduce heat to simmer, cover and cook 40 to 45 minutes or until barley is tender and liquid is absorbed. Fold Apples and parsley into barley mixture; cook 5 minutes and serve.

Makes 4 servings.

Notes:

German-Style Cooked Apple & Cabbage

I like informal food, maybe that's why I put hot mustard on my serving, with sausages, of course!

8 cups	**shredded red or green cabbage**	***2 L***
5 cups	**Apples peeled, cored and sliced**	***1.25 L***
4 cups	**boiling, salted water**	***1 L***
4	**slices bacon, diced**	***4***
1 cups	**sliced onion**	***250 mL***
2 tbsp	**cider vinegar**	***25 mL***
2 tbsp	**sugar**	***25 mL***
1/2 tsp	**dried fennel seed, crushed (optional)**	***2 mL***
1/4 tsp	**ground black pepper**	***1 mL***

In large saucepan combine cabbage, Apples and water; simmer 5 minutes or until cabbage is barely tender. Drain and remove cabbage and Apple mixture to serving bowl. In large saucepan, fry bacon and onion until onion is tender; stir in vinegar, sugar and fennel seed, if desired, and pepper. Cook 2 minutes. Pour bacon mixture over cabbage and Apple; mix lightly and serve.

Makes 6 servings.

Notes:

Roast Celery With Apples

Bold combinations lead to great dining!

1	**large garlic clove, crushed**	*1*
2 tbsp	**olive oil**	*25 mL*
1	**medium head celery (about 1-1/2 lbs.)**	*1*
2	**Apples, peeled, cored and quartered**	*2*
1 cups	**pure Apple juice**	*250 mL*
1/4 tsp	**ground cinnamon**	*1 mL*
1/4 tsp	**salt**	*1 mL*
1/8 tsp	**ground black pepper**	*.5 mL*
4	**slices toasted Italian bread**	*4*

Preheat oven to 375 degrees F. Place garlic and oil in a 13 x 9 x 2" baking pan; bake until oil is hot, about 5 minutes. Meanwhile trim base of celery; cut celery stalk crosswise, about 7 inches from base (save top for soups, stews, etc); cut stalk lengthwise into 4 wedges.

Place celery, Apples, Apple juice, cinnamon, salt and pepper in baking pan; bake, uncovered, until celery is crisp-tender, about 40 minutes, basting with pan juices every 10 to 15 minutes; discard garlic. Serve immediately over Italian bread.

Makes 4 servings.

Apple Carrot Casserole

Served with barbecued salmon steaks and a green salad, this unique dish will become one of your favourite spring dinners. Oh yes, and don't forget a nice chilled bottle of your favourite spicy white wine.

6	**large carrots**	***6***
5	**Apples**	***5***
5 tbsp	**sugar**	***75 mL***
5 tbsp	**flour**	***75 mL***
1/2 tsp	**nutmeg**	***2 mL***
1 tbsp	**margarine**	***15 mL***
1/2 cup	**orange juice**	***125 mL***

Slice carrots thinly and cook in salted water for 5 minutes; drain. Peel, core and slice Apples and cook in clear water 5 minutes; drain. Layer carrots and Apples in casserole. Mix sugar, flour and nutmeg; sprinkle on top. Dot with margarine. Pour orange juice over all. (Can be made ahead and baked just before serving). Bake 30-40 minutes in 350 degree F oven.

Makes 6 servings.

Notes:

Celery & Apple with Honey Mustard

We like this dish served with basmati rice, garnished with fresh coriander.

1 cup	**water, plus 2 tbsp**	***250 mL***
4 cups	**diagonally sliced celery cut 1/2 inch thick**	***1 L***
2 cups	**Apples, peeled, cored and diced**	***500 mL***
2 tbsp	**Dijon mustard**	***25 mL***
1 tbsp	**honey**	***15 mL***
1 tsp	**cornstarch**	***5 mL***
	pinch ground black pepper	
1/4 cup	**chopped toasted walnuts (optional)**	***50 mL***

In a large saucepan bring water to a boil. Add celery and Apples; cook and stir until crisp-tender, about 8 minutes. In a small bowl combine mustard, honey, cornstarch and black pepper with 2 tbsp of water. Add to celery mixture, stirring constantly; cook and stir until clear and thickened, about 1 minute. Stir in walnuts, if desired.

Makes 4 servings.

Notes:

Sweet & Sour Red Cabbage

My oldest son, Terry, makes terrific bratwurst sausages to go with this recipe. Served with a nice homemade hot mustard and fresh buns.... yummy.

1 cup	**water**	***250 mL***
1	**small head red cabbage (1 lb) shredded**	***1***
1	**Apple, unpeeled, cored, shredded**	***1***
1	**small potato, peeled, shredded**	***1***
1	**small onion, chopped**	***1***
	grated peel of 1/2 lemon	
	juice of 1 lemon	
3 tbsp	**brown sugar**	***45 mL***
1 tbsp	**red wine vinegar**	***15 mL***

In a large covered non-stick saucepan, cook cabbage, Apple, potato and onion in 1 cup water over low heat for 15 minutes; stir occasionally. Add remaining ingredients. Cover; cook over low heat 10 minutes longer, until vegetables are tender and mixture slightly thickens. Stir often.

Makes 6 servings.

Notes:

Curried Celery with Apples and Onions

Vegetables, fruit, curry and rice make a quick vegetarian meal that is really tasty.

1 tbsp	**vegetable oil**	*15 mL*
3 cups	**celery chopped**	*750 mL*
1 cup	**sweet red pepper chopped**	*250 mL*
3/4 cup	**onion chopped**	*175 mL*
2 tsp	**curry powder**	*10 mL*
1 1/2 cup	**Apples peeled, cored and cubed**	*375 mL*
3/4 cup	**pure Apple juice**	*175 mL*
1/2 tsp	**salt**	*2 mL*
2 cups	**steamed brown rice**	*500 mL*

In a large saucepan heat oil until hot. Add celery, red pepper and onion; cook and stir until barely crisp-tender, about 5 minutes. Add curry powder; cook 1 minute. Add Apple juice, Apples and salt; simmer, covered, until vegetables and Apples are tender, 2 to 3 minutes. Stir in steamed rice.

Makes 4 servings.

Notes:

Crunchy Apple Stir Fry

Vegetarians will enjoy this, but we like it served with medallions of pork.

1/2 cup	**sliced onion**	*125 mL*
2	**medium carrots, thinly sliced**	*2*
1 1/2 tsp	**olive oil**	*375 mL*
1 tsp	**crushed dried basil**	*5 mL*
1 cup	**snow pea pods**	*250 mL*
1 tbsp	**water**	*15 mL*
1/4 tsp	**ground ginger**	*1 mL*
1	**Apple, cored and thinly sliced**	*1*

In large saucepan, heat oil over medium-high heat; add onion, carrots, and basil; stir fry 3 minutes. Add pea pods, water, and ginger; stir fry 2 minutes. Add Apple and cook 2 minutes longer. Serve hot.

Makes 4 servings.

Notes:

Apple Pizza

For fun, use tortillas instead of pizza crust; the small ones make great individual servings, and let the kids 'decorate' their own!

1/2 cup	**low fat ricotta cheese**	*125 mL*
2 tbsp	**minced onion**	*25 mL*
1/2 tsp	**dried dill weed**	*2 mL*
1	**pre-cooked pizza crust**	*1*
2 cup	**Apples, cored and thinly sliced**	*500 mL*
1 cup	**red bell pepper, thinly sliced**	*250 mL*
3/4 cup	**shredded mozzarella cheese**	*175 mL*

Combine ricotta cheese, onion and dill; mix well. Spread on pizza crust. Layer Apples, and peppers on cheese mixture. Sprinkle with mozzarella cheese on top. Bake at 450 degrees F about 7 minutes or until mozzarella cheese melts and pizza is thoroughly heated.

Makes 6 servings.

Notes:

Apple Curry Rice

Golden Delicious is recommended. Try cooking the rice in 1/2 water and 1/2 pure Apple juice.

1/2 cup	**water**	*125 mL*
1/2 cup	**raisins (optional)**	*125 mL*
2 tbsp	**vegetable oil**	*25 mL*
1/2 cup	**chopped onion**	*125 mL*
2 tsp	**curry powder**	*10 mL*
1/2 tsp	**freshly ground black pepper**	*2 mL*
1	**Apple, peeled, cored, and chopped**	*1*
3 cups	**cooked brown rice**	*750 mL*
	salt to taste	

Boil the water and pour over the raisins in a bowl. Let them soak for 5 minutes. Drain, and set aside. Place the oil, onion, curry powder, and pepper in a 2-quart microwave-safe bowl and stir to combine. Microwave on high for 2 minutes, or until the onions are tender. Add the Apple tossing well to coat; stir in the rice. Re-cover and cook on high for 3 to 5 minutes, or until rice is heated through. Add the raisins. Re-cover and let stand for 2 minutes. Add salt to taste, if desired, and serve.

Makes 4 to 6 servings.

Apple & Brown Rice Pilaf

1/2	**onion, minced**	***1/2***
1 tbsp	**vegetable oil**	***15 mL***
1 1/2 cups	**quick cooking brown rice**	***375 mL***
1 1/4 cups	**chicken broth**	***300 mL***
1/2 tsp	**dried thyme, crushed**	***2 mL***
	salt and pepper to taste	
2 cups	**Apples, cored and diced**	***500 ml***
2 tbsp	**parsley, chopped**	***25 mL***

Sauté onion in oil in non-stick saucepan until tender; stir in rice and brown slightly. Stir in broth, thyme, salt and pepper; bring to boil. Cover tightly and reduce heat; simmer 15 minutes. Remove from heat; stir in Apples and parsley. Serve warm or cold.

Makes 4 servings.

Notes:

Spicy Apple Filled Squash

1	**acorn squash**	*1*
1	**Apple, peeled, cored and sliced**	*1*
2 tsp	**melted margarine**	*10 mL*
2 tsp	**packed brown sugar**	*10 mL*
1/8 tsp	**ground cinnamon**	*2 mL*
1/8 tsp	**ground nutmeg**	*2 mL*
	dash of ground cloves	

Heat oven to 350 degrees F. Grease a small baking dish. Halve squash and remove seeds; bake 35 minutes. Keep oven on. Cut squash halves in two; turn cut sides up. In small bowl, combine Apples, margarine, brown sugar, cinnamon, nutmeg and cloves and mix well. Top squash pieces with Apple mixture. Cover and bake 30 minutes or until Apples are tender. Serve.

Makes 4 servings.

Notes:

Squash & Apple Bake

The roadside markets near our home feature a wide variety of fresh Apples and squash in the fall. We can't help but stock up. And why not? They go so well together in recipes like this one.

2	**acorn squash**	*2*
1 tbsp	**vegetable oil**	*15 mL*
1 tbsp	**lemon juice**	*15 mL*
1	**Apple, cored and diced**	*1*
1	**medium leek, white part only, thinly sliced**	*1*
1/2 tsp	**salt**	*2 mL*
1/4 tsp	**ground cinnamon**	*1 mL*
1/4 tsp	**ground nutmeg**	*1 mL*
1/8 tsp	**ground allspice**	*.5 mL*
1/8 tsp	**ground white pepper**	*.5 mL*

Pierce the squash in 3 or 4 places with the tip of a sharp knife. Place the squash on a microwave dish and microwave on high for 4 minutes. Turn the squash and microwave on high for 4 to 6 minutes longer, or until it just begins to feel soft when gently squeezed. Let stand until cooled, about 5 minutes.

Meanwhile, in a 2-quart casserole dish, combine the oil, lemon juice, Apple, leek, salt, cinnamon, nutmeg, allspice, and pepper. Cover tightly with a lid or vented plastic wrap. Microwave on high for 5 minutes, or until the Apple and leek are quite soft.

Cut the squash in half and scoop out the seeds. Remove pulp to the casserole with the Apple mixture. Mash the squash with the back of a spoon while stirring in the Apple and leek to combine. Spoon the mixture back into the casserole dish. Cover loosely with plastic wrap. Microwave on high for 4 to 6 minutes, or until heated through.

Makes 4 servings.

Apple Glazed Sweet Potatoes

1/2 cups	**pure Apple juice**	*125 mL*
1/4 tsp	**cinnamon**	*1 mL*
1/2 tsp	**salt**	*2 mL*
6	**small sweet potatoes, cooked**	**6**

Slightly cook the sweet potatoes in the microwave on high. Cool, peel and slice. Pour Apple juice into a saucepan over low heat and stir in cinnamon and salt. Add sweet potatoes. Cook over low heat, turning sweet potatoes several times until they are well coated and most of the juice is absorbed, about 6 minutes.

Makes 6 servings.

Notes:

Apple Sage Dressing

Make this on its own, or as a fabulous stuffing for small poultry!

2 tsp	**vegetable oil**	*10 mL*
1 cup	**diced celery**	*250 mL*
1/2 cup	**diced onion**	*125 mL*
3	**slices whole wheat bread**	*3*
1 3/4 cups	**Apple cubed, unpeeled**	*450 mL*
2 tbsp	**chopped fresh parsley**	*25 mL*
2 tbsp	**currants**	*25 mL*
3/4 tsp	**rubbed sage**	*3 mL*
1/4 tsp	**salt**	*1 mL*
1/4 tsp	**dried whole thyme**	*1 mL*
1/8 tsp	**pepper**	*.5 mL*
1/3 cup	**pure Apple juice**	*75 mL*
	vegetable cooking spray	

Lightly toast the bread and cut into cubes. Heat oil in a small saucepan over medium-high heat until hot. Add the celery and onion and sauté for 7 minutes or until tender. Combine the bread cubes and the Apple, parsley, currants, sage, salt, thyme, and pepper in a large bowl and toss well. Add the celery mixture and Apple juice and stir well.

Spoon the mixture into a 1 1/2-quart casserole coated with cooking spray. Bake at 350 degrees F for 15 minutes. Stir gently and bake another 10 minutes or until top is crisp.

Makes 4 servings.

Picton Fair
FR
BOX McIntosh
Insert Flap Here
119
BLOOMFIELD
FOLD HERE AT PERFORATION
Picton Fair

Traditional Applesauce

Homemade Applesauce is a treat. There are many different ways to make it but at home, we always cook the Apples whole – skins, cores and all. This gives the Applesauce a pretty, pink blush. Once the Apples are cooked, we use a cone-shaped strainer with a cone-shaped wooden utensil and press the flesh from the skins and cores, then add the seasonings. However, if you peel and core the Apples before you cook them, you can add all the seasonings during the cooking process and purée in a food processor.*

3 lbs	**Apples, cored, and quartered and peeled***	***1.5 kg***
1/2 cup	**water**	***125 mL***
1	**lemon**	***1***
1/4 tsp	**cinnamon**	***1 mL***
1/4 tsp	**ground cloves**	***1 mL***
1/4 cup	**sugar or to taste**	***50 mL***

Combine all ingredients except the sugar in a large pot and bring to a boil. Lower heat, cover and simmer gently 12 - 15 minutes. Stir in sugar until dissolved. Remove from heat. Cool slightly. Process in a food processor or press through a sieve.

Makes about 5 cups.

Sauces

For the best butters, salsas, and sauces choose from:

Cortland
McIntosh
Golden Delicious
Russet
Northern Spy
Empire

Apple Clove Butter

In our home, Apples, oranges, cinnamon and cloves remind us all of Christmas – what a gift! Use 10 very pretty little jars to package this recipe and give to family and friends.

4 lbs	**Apples, peeled, cored, cut into 1-inch pieces**	***2.5 kg***
1 cup	**Apple cider**	***250 ml***
1/4 cup	**orange juice**	***50 mL***
1	**cinnamon stick, broken in half**	***1***
3/4 cup	**(packed) golden brown sugar**	***175 mL***
2 tsp	**grated orange peel**	***10 mL***
1/2 tsp	**ground cloves**	***2 mL***

Combine Apples, cider, orange juice and cinnamon stick in heavy large saucepan. Bring to boil. Reduce heat to medium-low. Cover and simmer until Apples are very tender, stirring occasionally, about 10 minutes. Discard cinnamon stick.

Purée Apple mixture in processor. Return to same saucepan. Stir in brown sugar, orange peel and cloves. Simmer over medium-low heat until mixture is dark in colour and thick, and mounds on spoon, stirring frequently, about 45 minutes. Transfer to large bowl. Cool completely. (Can be prepared 1 week ahead. Cover and refrigerate.)

Makes about 3 1/2 cups.

Apple Butter

Tradition! And tradition with taste; create a family memory. You can use ground cinnamon but the whole spice imparts a more subtle and pleasing flavour.

8 cups	**Apples peeled, cored, chopped**	*2 L*
1 cup	**Apple cider**	*250 mL*
	white sugar (1/3 cup - 75 mL - for every cup of processed sauce)	
	whole cinnamon stick	

Cook the Apples in cider over medium heat until soft. Process to sauce texture in food processor. Place the raw sauce in a large dutch oven or casserole. Add sugar and whole cinnamon. Bake at 300 degrees F for one hour.

Check for flavour and texture. The sauce should be thick and rich. Drop a spoonful onto a dish; if a puddle of juice forms around it in the next few seconds the sauce is not done yet.

Caution: If the sauce is cooked too long it becomes runny again and over-spicy. Place in sterile jars and process 15 minutes in boiling water bath.

Notes:

Dancin' Apple Salsa

Be creative with all our recipes, for example: tequila or white rum will give this salsa a finger snappin' twist! Use Golden Delicious for this recipe.

3	**Apples, cored and chopped**	*3*
2-4	**jalepeno peppers (or to taste)**	*2-4*
1/2 cup	**raisins (optional)**	*125 mL*
1/2 cup	**thinly sliced green onions**	*125 mL*
1/3 cup	**cider vinegar**	*75 mL*
3 tbsp	**brown sugar**	*45 mL*
1/4 tsp	**ground cumin**	*1 mL*

Combine Apples, peppers, raisins, onions, vinegar, sugar and cumin in medium bowl. Cover and chill at least 1 hour. Serve with grilled chicken or pork.

Makes 2 cups.

Notes:

Apple-Cherry Fruit Spread

Try this no-sugar, fat-free natural fruit purée on toast, muffins, waffles, and sandwiches.

3	**Apples, peeled, cored, and coarsely chopped**	*3*
1/2 cup	**dried cherries**	*125 mL*
1/2 cup	**fruit juice or water**	*125 mL*
1	**cinnamon stick**	*1*
1/2 tsp	**finely grated lemon zest**	*2 mL*

In medium saucepan, combine Apples, cherries, fruit juice, and cinnamon stick. Cover and bring to simmer over medium heat; cook 15 minutes, stirring frequently. Uncover and reduce heat to low; cook 15 to 20 minutes longer or until Apples are very soft but retain their shape.

Remove cinnamon stick. Add lemon zest to Apple mixture. In blender or food processor, purée Apple mixture until chunky spread forms. Cool completely. Chill before serving. Store in refrigerator.

Makes 1 1/2 cups.

Cashmere Chutney

2 lb	**Apples**	*1 kg*
	vinegar (as much as needed to cover)	
1/2 tsp	**cayenne pepper**	*2 mL*
1/2 cup	**whole ginger, chopped and pounded**	*125 g*
2 lbs	**brown sugar**	*1 kg*
1 lb	**raisins**	*500 g*
1/4 cup	**salt**	*50 g*
1 lb	**dates**	*500 g*
1	**clove garlic**	*1*
1/4 tsp	**ground cloves**	*1 mL*

Put Apples chopped and cored, but not peeled in preserving pan. Cover with vinegar. Cook until soft.

Add the cayenne, ginger, brown sugar, raisins, salt, dates, clove, and garlic. Boil half an hour. Immediately fill hot, sterilized pint canning jars with mixture, leaving 1/2-inch headspace. Carefully run a non-metallic utensil down inside of jars to remove trapped air bubbles. Wipe jar tops and threads clean. Place lids on jars and screw on bands tightly. Process in boiling water bath for 15 minutes. Keep twelve months before using.

Notes:

Cranberry-Apple Chutney

We have one family member who won't eat raisins, so we consider raisins (and currants) to be optional in all our recipes.

3 cups	**Apples, peeled and diced**	***750 mL***
1 cup	**cranberries**	***250 mL***
1-1/4 cup	**sugar**	***310 mL***
1 cup	**brown sugar**	***250 mL***
1 cup	**golden raisins**	***250 mL***
1/2 cup	**coarsely chopped walnuts or pecans**	***125 mL***
1/2 cup	**cider vinegar**	***125 mL***
1	**orange, sliced very thin and halved**	***1***
1/4 tsp	**mace**	***1 mL***
1/4 tsp	**curry powder**	***1 mL***
1/4 tsp	**cloves**	***1 mL***
1/4 tsp	**allspice**	***1 mL***
1/4 cup	**preserved ginger, chopped**	***1 mL***
4	**cloves garlic, peeled**	***4***
1	**large onion, chopped**	***1***
1/2 tsp	**salt**	***2 mL***
1/4 tsp	**mustard seed**	***1 mL***

Combine all ingredients in a large heavy saucepan and bring to a rolling boil, stirring constantly. Reduce heat and simmer, uncovered, stirring occasionally, until Apples are tender and the syrup is very thick, almost caramelized.

Immediately fill hot, sterilized pint canning jars with mixture, leaving 1/2-inch headspace. Carefully run a non-metallic utensil down inside of jars to remove trapped air bubbles. Wipe jar tops and threads clean. Place lids on jars and screw on bands tightly. Process in boiling water bath for 15 minutes. Cool and store in refrigerator after opening.

Makes about 7 jars.

Apple, Pear And Raisin Chutney

You can mix and match the Apple varieties here.

4	**red Bartlett pears**	***4***
4	**Apples**	***4***
1	**orange, unpeeled, seeded, chopped**	***1***
1	**lemon, unpeeled, seeded, chopped**	***1***
1/2	**lime, unpeeled, seeded, chopped**	***1/2***
1/2 cup	**light brown sugar, packed**	***125 mL***
1/2 cup	**granulated sugar**	***125 mL***
1/2 cup	**water**	***125 mL***
1/4 cup	**cider vinegar**	***60 mL***
2 tbsp	**fresh lemon juice**	***25 mL***
1 cup	**raisins**	***250 mL***

Quarter and core 2 pears and 2 Apples. Place in food processor with orange, lemon and lime and pulse until finely chopped. Transfer to heavy saucepan, add sugars, water and vinegar and bring to boil. Lower heat and simmer 30-35 minutes until thickened.

Meanwhile, core and dice remaining Apples and pears, place in bowl and cover with water and lemon juice. When cooked mixture is thickened, drain and rinse the diced fruit and add to saucepan with raisins. Heat for 3 minutes, then allow to cool.

Transfer to glass container with tight fitting lid and refrigerate or immediately fill hot, sterilized pint canning jars with mixture, leaving 1/2-inch headspace. Carefully run a non-metallic utensil down inside of jars to remove trapped air bubbles. Wipe jar tops and threads clean. Place lids on jars and screw on bands tightly. Process in boiling water bath for 15 minutes.

Makes about 8 cups.

Apple Chutney

Northern Spys or Empires would be your first choice here, but McIntosh or Golden Delicious will do just fine.

8 cups	**Apples**	*2 L*
1 cup	**chopped onion**	*250 mL*
1 cup	**chopped red bell peppers**	*250 mL*
2	**hot red or green chiles**	*2*
1 clove	**garlic, minced**	*1*
1-1/2 lbs	**raisins**	*750 g*
4 cups	**firmly packed brown sugar**	*1 L*
3 tbsp	**mustard seed**	*50 mL*
2 tbsp	**ground ginger**	*25 mL*
2 tsp	**ground allspice**	*10 mL*
2 tsp	**salt**	*10 mL*
4 cups	**cider vinegar**	*1 L*

Peel, core and chop about 10 medium Apples to get 8 cups. Seed and mince the chiles.

Combine all ingredients in a 6 to 8-quart stainless steel saucepan or pot. Bring to a boil, reduce heat and simmer, uncovered for 1 to 1-1/2 hour or until dark brown and thick, stirring occasionally at the beginning and constantly at the end.

Immediately fill hot, sterilized pint canning jars with mixture, leaving 1/2-inch headspace. Carefully run a non-metallic utensil down inside of jars to remove trapped air bubbles. Wipe jar tops and threads clean. Place lids on jars and screw on bands tightly. Process in boiling water bath for 15 minutes.

Makes 4-5 pints.

Jellied Apple Cranberry Sauce

Try this sauce with turkey instead of just plain cranberry sauce.

1 12-oz	**bag of cranberries, picked over**	*1*
2	**Apples**	*2*
1 cup	**dry white wine**	*250 mL*
1 1/2 cups	**sugar**	*375 mL*
	mint sprigs for garnish	

In a large saucepan combine the cranberries, the Apples, chopped coarse (not peeled or cored), the wine, and the sugar, bring the mixture to a boil, stirring, and simmer it, covered, stirring occasionally, for 15 minutes.

Simmer the mixture, uncovered, stirring occasionally, for 20 to 25 minutes more, or until it is very thick and is reduced to about 3 cups.

Force the mixture through a food mill fitted with the fine disk into a bowl, spoon it into an oiled 3- to 4-cup decorative mold, and chill covered, overnight.

Run a thin knife around the edge of the mold and dip the mold into warm water for 10 seconds. Invert the mold onto a serving plate and garnish the cranberry saucc with the mint sprigs.

Makes 8 servings.

Missing Persons Hot Sauce

This sauce is absolutely marvellous with roast lamb, goose, or pork. Control the 'heat' by the numbers (and types) of hot peppers you use. Any of your favourite sauce Apples can be used. (This sauce placed in the 'top 20' at the 2nd Annual Hot Sauce Contest in Kingston, Ontario, 1999.)

		2
2	**Apples**	*1*
1	**whole garlic**	*1*
1	**onion**	*3*
3	**hot yellow peppers**	*3*
3	**jalepeno peppers**	*50 mL*
1/4 cup	**maple syrup**	*50 mL*
1/4 cup	**vinegar**	*50 mL*
1/4 cup	**bourbon**	*2*
2	**drops almond extract**	*2 mL*
1/2 tsp	**salt**	*25 mL*
1 tbsp	**olive oil**	

Core the Apples, peel the onion and cut the top off the garlic bulb to expose the cloves. Bake the Apples, garlic, onion, hot yellow peppers and jalepeno peppers in a 375 degree F oven. Check frequently and remove each item as it becomes soft. Do not overroast.

Peel Apples, squeeze out garlic cloves from casing and place in blender. Wearing gloves, clean the hot yellow peppers and jalepenos, discarding tops and seeds, leaving skin and pulp. Add the roasted onion and peppers to the blender.

Add maple syrup, vinegar, bourbon and almond extract. Purée until well-blended. Heat olive oil and salt in a small pot. Add sauce from blender and simmer for 5 to 7 minutes to meld flavours. Keep refrigerated, but serve at room temperature.

Microwave Chunky Applesauce

This is a quick way to make Applesauce. If you want it smooth, buzz it for a few seconds in a food processor. Any of the Apples best suited for sauces can be used. So try Empire, Northern Spy, Golden Delicious, McIntosh or Cortland. You can increase the water and/or sugar to get your preferred consistency and sweetness.

8	**Apples, pared, cored and cut into chunks**	*8*
1/3 cup	**water**	*75 mL*
1/4 cup	**sugar**	*50 mL*
1/8 tsp	**ground cinnamon**	*.5 mL*
	dash ground nutmeg	

Combine Apples and water in 2-quart microwave-safe dish. Cover and microwave on high (100%) 12 to 14 minutes or until Apples are tender; stir 2 to 3 times during cooking. Stir in remaining ingredients; cover. Microwave on high 2 to 4 minutes or until sugar dissolves. Stir well.

Makes 4 1/2 cups.

Notes:

Peach & Apple Salsa

This salsa is very nice with your favourite grilled chicken recipe and it can be made hours ahead and chilled.

2	**large ripe but firm peaches**	***2***
1 small	**Apple, peeled, cored, chopped**	***1***
1/2 cup	**chopped fresh cilantro**	***125 mL***
1/4 cup	**honey**	***125 mL***
2 tbsp	**fresh lime juice**	***25 mL***
1/4 tsp	**ground allspice**	***1 mL***
1/4 tsp	**ground cinnamon**	***1 mL***

Bring medium saucepan of water to boil over high heat. Add peaches; cook 30 seconds. Using slotted spoon, transfer peaches to bowl of cold water. Drain peaches. Peel and chop coarsely. Place peaches in large bowl. Mix in all remaining ingredients.

Notes:

When cooking with Apples, choose from:

Empire
Northern Spy
Spartan
Golden Delicious

Cottage-Style Braised Chicken

Homey, hearty and flavorful, this one-plate meal needs only bread (try raisin or olive), a salad (sparked with citrus) and a full-bodied wine.

1/4 cup	**all-purpose white flour**	***50 mL***
8	**4-ounce boneless, skinless chicken breasts**	***8***
3 tsp	**vegetable oil**	***15 mL***
	salt & freshly ground black pepper to taste	
2	**onions, coarsely chopped**	***2***
1 cup	**Apple cider**	***250 mL***
1	**large rutabaga, peeled and cut into 1/4-inch-by-2-inch julienne**	***1***
1 cup	**chicken broth**	***250 mL***
4	**firm ripe pears, peeled, cored & diced**	***4***
1/4 cup	**fresh lemon juice**	***50 mL***
1 tbsp	**chopped fresh thyme or 1 teaspoon dried thyme leaves**	***15 mL***

Dredge chicken breasts in flour to coat, shaking off excess. Reserve unused flour. In a 6-quart Dutch oven, heat 1 tsp oil over medium-high heat. Sauté chicken breasts until golden, about 3 minutes per side. Remove to a plate, lightly salt and pepper, and set aside.

Reduce heat to medium-low. Heat the remaining 1 tsp of oil and add onions. Stir until golden brown. Add the reserved flour and stir 1 minute more. Gradually add Apple cider and stir until thickened, about 2 minutes. Add rutabaga and chicken broth. Bring to a simmer, reduce heat to low; cover and simmer until the rutabaga is tender, 15 to 20 minutes. Stir in lemon juice, thyme and diced pears. Lay the reserved chicken on top and cover the pan. Cook until the chicken is no longer pink in the center and the pears are tender, 5 to 6 minutes more.

Makes 8 servings.

Apple Turkey Gyro

A fine fistfull of flavourful food!

1 tbsp	**vegetable oil**	***15 mL***
1 cup	**sliced onion**	***250 mL***
1 cup	**thinly sliced sweet red pepper**	***250 mL***
1 cup	**thinly sliced sweet green pepper**	***250 mL***
2 tbsp	**lemon juice**	***25 mL***
1/2 lb	**cooked turkey breast, cut in strips**	***250 g***
1	**Apple, cored and finely chopped**	***1***
6	**pocket pita bread, warmed**	***6***
1/2 cup	**plain yogurt**	***125 mL***

In large saucepan, heat oil over medium heat. Add onion, peppers, and lemon juice and cook until tender-crisp. Stir in turkey and Apple; cook until turkey is heated through. Remove from heat. Fill each pita with some of mixture; drizzle with yogurt. Serve warm.

Makes 4 servings.

Notes:

St. David's Chicken with Apples and Leeks

4	boneless, skinless chicken breasts	4
3 tsp	olive oil	15 mL
	salt & freshly ground black pepper to taste	
2	large leeks, white parts only, washed and cut into julienne strips (2 cups)	2
2	large cloves garlic, minced	2
1 tbsp	sugar	15 mL
2 tsp	minced fresh rosemary or 1/2 tsp dried	10 mL
1/4 cup	cider vinegar	50 mL
2	Apples, peeled, cored and thinly sliced	2
1 cup	chicken broth	250 mL

Place chicken breasts between 2 sheets of plastic wrap. Use a rolling pin or a small heavy pot to pound them to a thickness of 1/4 inch. In a large nonstick saucepan, heat 1 1/2 tsp of the oil over medium-high heat. Season the chicken breasts with salt and pepper and add to the pan. Cook until browned on both sides, about 3 minutes per side. Transfer to a plate and keep warm.

Reduce the heat to low. Add the remaining 1 1/2 tsp oil and leeks. Cook, stirring, until the leeks are soft, about 5 minutes. Add garlic, sugar and rosemary and cook until fragrant, about 2 minutes more. Increase the heat to medium-high, stir in vinegar and cook until most of the liquid has evaporated.

Add Apples and chicken broth and cook, stirring once or twice, until the Apples are tender, about 3 minutes. Taste and adjust seasonings with salt and pepper. Reduce the heat to low and return the chicken and any juices to the saucepan. Simmer gently until the chicken is heated through.

Makes 4 servings.

September Chicken

When this is cooking, the kitchen fills with delicious aromas to whet your appetite.

6	**boneless, skinless chicken breasts**	*6*
1	**sliced onion**	*1*
1	**10 oz can condensed chicken broth**	*1*
3 tbsp	**Apple cider or pure Apple juice**	*45 mL*
3	**Apples, cored and sliced**	*3*
6-8	**artichoke hearts, cut in half**	*6-8*
	pinch of ground cinnamon, nutmeg, salt and pepper	
	minced fresh dill or parsley	

Spray a large non-stick saucepan with cooking spray. Brown chicken breasts on both sides. Remove chicken from saucepan and set aside. Stir in sliced onion, Apples, artichokes, broth, juice and spices. Cook 3 minutes. Spread chicken breasts in saucepan; arrange Apples, onion and artichokes on top. Simmer, covered, about 10 minutes or until chicken is tender and heated through. Sprinkle with salt and pepper. Garnish with fresh parsley or dill and Apple slices before serving.

Makes 6 servings.

Notes:

Apple Chicken Stir-Fry

Use your imagination with this one. If you enjoy Asian cooking, you know that whatever you find in the bottom of the crisper bin of the refrigerator is fair game. Makes a great outdoor summer Saturday lunch with a tumbler of cold Apple cider and good friends. Use whatever Apple makes you smile!

1/4 cup	**pure Apple juice or cider**	***50 mL***
2 tbsp	**cornstarch**	***25 mL***
1 lb	**cubed boneless, skinless, chicken breast**	***500 g***
1/2 cup	**onion, vertically sliced**	***125 mL***
1 cup	**(2 medium) carrots, thinly sliced**	***250 mL***
1 1/2 tsp	**vegetable oil**	***7 mL***
1 tsp	**dried basil, crushed**	***5 mL***
1 cup	**fresh or frozen Chinese pea pods**	***250 mL***
1	**Apple cored and thinly sliced**	***1***
1 tbsp	**olive oil**	***15 mL***
4 cups	**cooked rice**	***1 L***

Add corn starch to cider/juice, blend and set aside.

Stir fry cubed chicken breast in 1 tbsp olive oil in nonstick saucepan until lightly browned and cooked. Remove from saucepan.

Stir-fry onion, carrots and basil in oil in same saucepan until carrots are tender. Stir in pea pods and juice/cornstarch mixture; stir-fry 2 minutes. Remove from heat; stir in Apples. Add chicken, serve hot over cooked rice.

Makes 4 servings.

Chicken Oriental Kabobs

Present this attractive entree on a large platter of steaming rice.

4	**whole chicken breasts**	***4***
8	**fresh mushrooms**	***8***
8	**parboiled whole white onions**	***8***
2	**oranges, quartered**	***2***
8	**canned pineapple chunks**	***8***
8	**cherry tomatoes**	***8***
1 cup	**Apple cider**	***1***
1 cup	**dry white wine**	***250 mL***
2 tbsp	**soy sauce, low-sodium**	***25 mL***
	dash of ground ginger	
	pepper to taste	
2 tbsp	**vinegar**	***25 mL***
1/4 cup	**olive oil**	***50 mL***

Remove bones and skin from chicken. Cut each half chicken breast into 4 pieces. Sprinkle with pepper. Thread 8 bamboo or metal skewers as follows: chicken, mushroom, chicken, onion, chicken, orange quarter, chicken, pineapple chunk, cherry tomato. If you are using bamboo skewers don't forget to soak them in water for 20 minutes before you use them.

Place kabobs in shallow pan. Combine remaining ingredients; spoon over kabobs. Marinate in refrigerator at least 1 hour. Drain, reserving liquids. Broil 6" from heat, 15 minutes on each side, brushing with marinade every 5 minutes.

Makes 8 servings.

Regimental Chicken

The troops will love this!

4	**strips of bacon, cut into 1/2-inch dice**	***4***
1 tbsp	**canola oil**	***15 mL***
1	**3-to-3 1/2-lb. chicken, cut into 8 pieces,**	***1***
	salt & freshly ground black pepper to taste	
4	**large onions, thinly sliced**	***4***
1	**clove garlic, finely chopped**	***1***
3 cups	**hard Apple cider**	***750 mL***
1/3 cup	**brandy**	***75 mL***
1	**bouquet garni in a cheesecloth bag:** **6 sprigs parsley,** **4 sprigs fresh thyme or** **1/2 tsp dried thyme leaves, and** **2 bay leaves**	***1***

Preheat oven to 325 degrees F. In a deep ovenproof frying pan with a lid, brown bacon over medium-high heat, about 3 minutes, and transfer to paper towels to drain. Pour off any fat in the pan. Add 1/2 tbsp of the oil to the pan and brown chicken over high heat, about 3 minutes per side. Transfer the chicken to a plate, season with salt and pepper and set aside.

Add the remaining 1/2 tbsp oil to the pan, reduce heat to low and add onions. Cook, stirring occasionally, until the onions are very tender and golden. Stir in garlic and cook for 1 minute. Pour in cider and brandy and bring to a boil. Add bouquet garni and the reserved bacon and chicken. Cover and bake until the chicken is very tender and no longer pink inside, 45 minutes to 1 hour. Remove the bouquet garni.

Makes 6 servings.

Apple-Ginger Chicken

We enjoy this dish with Asian noodles and a hot pepper sate sauce.

2	**cloves garlic, finely chopped**	*2*
1 tbsp	**finely chopped fresh ginger**	*15 mL*
1 tsp	**ground coriander**	*5 mL*
1 tsp	**ground cumin**	*5 mL*
1 tsp	**whole yellow mustard seeds**	*5 mL*
1 lb	**boneless, skinless chicken breasts, fat trimmed, cut into 1/4-inch-thick slices**	*500 g*
1 tbsp	**all-purpose white flour**	*15 mL*
1 1/2 tsp	**canola oil**	*7 mL*
1	**Apple, cored and cut into thin wedges**	*1*
3/4 cup	**chicken stock**	*175 mL*
	salt to taste	
1 tbsp	**chopped fresh cilantro or parsley**	**15 mL**

In a small bowl, stir together garlic, ginger, coriander, cumin and mustard seeds; set aside. In a medium-sized bowl, toss chicken with flour until evenly coated. In a large nonstick saucepan or wok over high heat, heat 1 tsp of the oil. Add the chicken and sauté until well-browned on all sides, about 4 minutes. With a slotted spoon, transfer the chicken to a plate and set aside.

Add the remaining 1/2 tsp oil and Apples to the pan. Reduce heat to medium and cook, stirring, until Apples arc lightly browned, about 3 minutes. Reduce heat to medium-low and add the reserved spice mixture. Stir until the Apples are tender and the garlic is fragrant, 2 to 3 minutes. Add chicken stock and the reserved chicken; increase heat to high.

Bring the mixture to a simmer and cook until the sauce is slightly thickened and the chicken is no longer pink inside, about 2 minutes. Season with salt. Transfer to a serving dish and sprinkle with cilantro or parsley.

Grilled Mustard Chicken

A distinctive blend of three mustards keeps these chicken breasts moist and tasty.

1/4 cup	**Dijon mustard**	***50 mL***
1/4 cup	**coarse-grain (stone-ground) mustard**	***50 mL***
1/4 cup	**German mustard**	***50 mL***
1/4 cup	**white vinegar**	***50 mL***
1/3 cup	**Apple cider**	***75 mL***
2 tbsp	**fresh lemon juice**	***25 mL***
1/4 tsp	**grated lemon zest**	***1 mL***
1	**shallot, peeled and thinly sliced**	***5 mL***
1	**clove garlic, minced**	***5 mL***
	freshly ground black pepper	***5 mL***
	vegetable oil for brushing grill	
4	**boneless, skinless chicken breasts**	***4***

In a shallow stainless steel dish, combine mustards, vinegar, cider, juices, zest, shallots, garlic and pepper. Add chicken and turn to coat. Cover and marinate for 2 to 4 hours in the refrigerator, turning occasionally.

Shortly before serving, prepare a charcoal fire or preheat a gas grill. Remove chicken from marinade, discard marinade, and cook chicken on a lightly oiled grill for about 3 to 4 minutes per side, or until no longer pink inside.

Makes 4 servings.

Apple Turkey Sauté

1/2 cup	**unsifted all-purpose flour**	*125 mL*
1/2 tsp	**salt**	*2 mL*
1/4 tsp	**ground black pepper**	*1 mL*
1 lb	**turkey breast, cut into 1/4 inch thick slices**	*500 g*
1 tbsp	**margarine**	*15 mL*
2 tbsp	**olive oil**	*25 mL*
3	**Apples, peeled, cored and sliced**	*3*
1/2 cup	**sliced mushrooms**	*125 mL*
1/2 cup	**sliced onion**	*125 mL*
2 tbsp	**capers**	*25 mL*
1 cup	**Apple juice**	*250 mL*
2 tbsp	**chopped fresh parsley leaves**	*25 mL*

In small bowl, combine flour, salt and pepper; dredge turkey slices in flour mixture to lightly coat. In large saucepan heat margarine and olive oil over medium heat; add dredged turkey slices and cook, turning, until browned on both sides and cooked through. Remove turkey from saucepan and keep warm.

Add Apples, mushrooms, onion and capers to saucepan, sauté just until Apples are tender. Stir in juice to deglaze saucepan and simmer 5 minutes. Arrange turkey on platter, cover with Apple and vegetable mixture. Spoon sauce in pan over all, garnish with parsley and serve.

Makes 6 servings.

Turkey Kielbasa & Sauerkraut Potpie

Using kielbasa made with turkey is a good way to trim the fat content for our health and enjoyment of life.

Filling

1 tsp	**olive oil**	*5 mL*
2	**onions, thinly sliced (2 cups)**	*2*
2	**cloves**	*2*
2 tsp	**garlic, minced**	*10 mL*
1 tbsp	**chopped fresh thyme or 1 tsp dried thyme leaves**	*15 mL*
3 tbsp	**all-purpose white flour**	*50 mL*
1 1/2 cups	**chicken broth**	*375 mL*
3/4 cup	**Apple cider**	*175 mL*
2 1/2 cups	**diced cooked turkey or chicken**	*750 mL*
1/2 pound	**turkey kielbasa, sliced 1/4-inch thick**	*250 g*
2 cups	**sauerkraut, rinsed and squeezed dry**	*500 mL*
2 tbsp	**grainy mustard**	*25 mL*
	Salt & freshly ground black pepper to taste	

Topping

2	**large egg whites**	*2*
1/4 cup	**low-fat milk**	*50 mL*
1/4	**teaspoon salt**	*50 mL*
1	**loaf unsliced seeded rye bread crust trimmed, cubed (8 cups)**	*1*

To Make Filling:

Preheat oven to 350 degrees F. In a large saucepan or Dutch oven, heat oil over medium heat. Add onions and cook, stirring occasionally, until softened but not browned, about 5 minutes. Add cloves, garlic and thyme and cook until fragrant, about 1 minute more.

Add flour and cook, stirring constantly, until the flour starts to turn golden, about 2 minutes. Stir in chicken broth and cider and bring to a simmer, stirring constantly, until the sauce thickens, about 5 minutes. Remove from the heat and add turkey or chicken, turkey kielbasa, sauerkraut and mustard; season with salt and pepper. Transfer to a deep 10-inch pie pan or other 2-quart baking dish and set aside.

To Make Topping:
In a large bowl, whisk together egg whites, milk and salt. Add bread cubes and toss to coat. Scatter over the top of the filling. Set the baking dish on a baking sheet and bake for 25 to 30 minutes, or until the topping is golden and the filling is bubbling.

Notes:

Fish & Seafood

When cooking with Apples, choose from:
Empire
Northern Spy
Spartan
Golden Delicious

Cider Mussels

Serve as an appetizer. Grant Howes of The County Cider Company provided this recipe.

1	**large onion diced**	*1*
1 tbsp	**butter**	*15 mL*
1 tbsp	**sugar**	*15 mL*
1 litre	**Apple cider**	*1 L*
1/2 tsp	**caraway seed**	*2 mL*
2 lbs	**mussels**	*1 kg*
	pinch salt	

Sauté diced onion and butter in saucepan until lightly browned. Add sugar and caramelize. Add 1/4 litre cider to mixture and reduce to a relish consistency. Reserve.

In large saucepan, combine remaining cider and caraway seed and bring to a boil. Add mussels and salt to liquid and cover. Once shells open, (3-5 minutes) remove mussels from cider and chill immediately. Half shell mussels. Increase heat on remaining cider and reduce liquid to the consistency of syrup. Remove from heat.

Spoon syrup over mussels on half shell and top with relish and serve either chilled or immediately.

Makes 4 servings.

Apple Stuffed Cod Fillets

2 tbsp	**olive oil**	***25 mL***
1 cup	**Apple, grated and peeled**	***250 mL***
1/2 cup	**grated carrot**	***125 mL***
1/2 cup	**minced green onion**	***125 mL***
2 tbsp	**fresh lemon juice**	***25 mL***
1/4 tsp	**ground ginger**	***1 mL***
1/4 tsp	**ground mustard**	***1 mL***
1/4 tsp	**salt**	***1 mL***
1/4 tsp	**ground black pepper**	***1 mL***
1/8 tsp	**dried thyme**	***.5 mL***
4	**sole, cod or other white fish fillets (4-5 ounces each)**	***4***
1/4 cups	**chicken broth or water**	***50 mL***

Heat oven to 400 degrees F; lightly oil small roasting pan. In medium-size bowl, combine Apple, carrot, green onion, lemon juice, ginger, mustard, salt, pepper and thyme; mix well. Spread Apple mixture evenly over length of fillets; carefully roll up.

Place stuffed fillets, seam side down, in oiled pan. Pour broth over rolled fillets; cover with aluminum foil and bake 10-15 minutes, or until fish is opaque and barely flakes. Serve.

Makes 4 servings.

Broiled Salmon with Apple Date Chutney

Steamed green beans and a rice or pasta salad from the deli go nicely with this entree. End with a simple but sophisticated dessert of coffee ice cream drizzled with brandy and sprinkled with toasted hazelnuts. Choose your favourite tart Apple!

2	**1-inch-thick salmon steaks**	***2***
6 tsp	**olive oil**	***90 mL***
1 1/2 tsp	**curry powder**	***7 mL***
2/3 cup	**chopped red onion**	***160 mL***
3/4 cup	**chopped peeled tart Apple**	***175 mL***
1/4 cup	**chopped pitted dates**	***50 mL***
2 tbsp	**Apple juice**	***25 mL***
1 tbsp	**white wine vinegar**	***15 mL***

Preheat broiler. Brush each salmon steak with 1 tsp oil. Sprinkle each with 1/4 tsp curry powder, salt and pepper. Broil salmon until just opaque in centre, about 5 minutes per side.

Meanwhile, heat remaining 4 tsp oil in heavy medium saucepan over medium-low heat. Add onion and sauté until onion begins to soften, about 3 minutes. Mix in Apple, dates, Apple juice and remaining 1 tsp curry powder. Cook 2 minutes longer. Mix in vinegar; simmer 1 minute. Season chutney to taste with salt and pepper.

Transfer salmon to plates. Spoon chutney alongside and serve.

Makes 2 servings.

Lobster with Curry Sauce

The Apple brandy lifts the sauce to a higher level of elegance.

2 - 1 3/4 lb	**whole live lobsters**	*2*
4 tbsp	**butter**	*60 mL*
1 cup	**chopped onion**	*250 mL*
1 1/2 tbsp	**curry powder**	*22 mL*
1 tbsp	**chopped garlic**	*15 mL*
1 tbsp	**tomato paste**	*15 mL*
1/4 cup	**Apple brandy**	*50 mL*
1 cup	**dry white wine**	*250 mL*
3	**fresh thyme sprigs or 1 teaspoon dried**	*3*
3	**fresh parsley sprigs**	*3*
1	**bay leaf**	*1*
2 1/2 tbsp	**all purpose flour**	*35 mL*

Bring large pot of water to boil. Add lobsters; cover and boil 9 minutes. Using tongs, transfer lobsters to large bowl of cold water. Reserve 4 cups cooking liquid. Drain lobsters. Working over bowl to collect juices, remove claws and tails. Cut tail meat through shells into 1/2-inch-wide medallions. Remove shells. Crack claws; carefully remove meat. Reserve medallions and claw meat. Cut shells into large pieces, reserving all juices and shells.

Melt 1 tbsp butter in heavy large saucepan over medium heat. Add onion, curry and garlic; sauté 2 minutes. Stir in tomato paste, then Apple brandy and reserved shells and juices. Boil mixture 2 minutes. Add reserved 4 cups lobster cooking liquid, wine, thyme, parsley and bay leaf; bring to boil. Reduce heat; simmer until sauce is reduced to 1 2/3 cups, about 45 minutes. Strain into medium saucepan, discarding solids. (Can be prepared 6 hours ahead. Cover; chill lobster and sauce.)

Mix 2 1/2 tbsps butter and flour in small bowl. Bring sauce to simmer. Whisk in butter mixture; boil 2 minutes, whisking constantly. Season with salt and pepper. Melt 1 tbsp butter in another heavy medium saucepan over medium heat. Add lobster medallions and claw meat. Sauté just until heated through, about 1 minute. Divide sauce among 4 plates. Arrange medallions and claw meat on top of sauce and serve.

Makes 4 appetizer servings or 2 main-course servings

Apple Halibut Kebabs

1/2 cup	**dry white wine**	***125 mL***
4 tsp	**olive oil**	***20 mL***
2 tbsp	**lime juice**	***25 mL***
2 tbsp	**finely chopped onion**	***25 mL***
1/2 tsp	**salt**	***2 mL***
1/2 tsp	**dried thyme, crushed**	***2 mL***
1/8 tsp	**pepper**	***.5 mL***
1 cup	**Apple cored and cut in 1 inch cubes**	***250 mL***
1	**medium green or sweet red pepper, cut in 1 inch squares**	***1***
1	**small onion, cut in 1 inch squares and separated**	***1***
1 lb	**halibut, cut in 1 to 1 1/2 inch cubes**	***500 g***

Note: Soak bamboo skewers in water for 20 minutes before using.

Combine wine, oil, lime juice, chopped onion, salt, thyme and pepper; mix well. Marinate remaining ingredients in mixture 1-2 hours. Thread Apple, pepper, onion and halibut on long metal or bamboo skewers; repeat five times on each skewer, ending with Apple. Broil or grill 4-5 inches from heat 6-8 minutes or until fish flakes when tested with a fork. Serve warm or cold.

Makes 4 servings.

Red Snapper with Gingered Apple and Cabbage

The zesty flavour of a spiced and pickled cabbage-Apple mixture makes an ideal accompaniment to tender herbed snapper.

2 tsp	**canola oil**	*10 mL*
2 tbsp	**finely chopped fresh ginger**	*25 mL*
4 cups	**packed thinly sliced red cabbage**	*1 L*
1/2 tsp	**salt**	*2 mL*
1 tbsp	**cider vinegar**	*15 mL*
1 tsp	**sugar**	*5 mL*
1	**Apple, cored and sliced**	*1*
4	**red snapper fillets (6-ounces each)**	*4*
1 cup	**milk**	*250 mL*
1 cup	**finely ground fresh bread crumbs**	*250 mL*
1 tbsp	**finely chopped fresh parsley**	*15 mL*
1 tbsp	**butter**	*15 mL*

In large, nonstick saucepan, heat oil over medium heat. Add ginger and sauté 2 minutes. Add cabbage and 1/4 tsp salt; reduce heat to low, cover and cook, stirring occasionally for 20 minutes. Stir in vinegar and sugar; transfer to bowl to cool. In microwave-safe dish, cover sliced Apple with waxed paper and microwave on high (100 %) 1 minute or until softened. Set aside.

Cut each fillet crosswise diagonally into three strips; soak fish strips in milk. In shallow bowl, combine bread crumbs, parsley, and remaining 1/4 tsp salt. Heat butter over medium-low heat in saucepan. Dip fish strips in bread crumb mixture to coat; add to saucepan and sauté 6 to 8 minutes, turning to brown evenly and cook through. To serve, toss Apple slices with cabbage; mound mixture in centre of each serving plate. Arrange fish strips around each mound of Apple mixture.

Makes 4 servings.

Cider Poached Trout

Another great from The County Cider Company, thanks Grant!

4	**fillets of trout**	***4***
3/4 litre	**Apple cider**	***3/4 L***
1	**stalk celery chopped**	***1***
1	**small onion chopped**	***1***
1 tbsp	**cracked pepper**	***15 mL***
1	**bay leaf**	***1***
3 tbsp	**heavy cream**	***45 mL***
1/2 cup	**butter**	***125 mL***

In a large saucepan, combine cider, celery, onion, pepper and bay leaf and bring to a boil. Reduce heat to a rolling boil and place fillets in pan, skin side down. Poach until fish is just cooked - about 4 minutes. Remove fish and keep warm.

Strain liquid and on high heat reduce liquid to a syrup consistency. Add cream and bring to a boil. Remove from heat and gradually whisk in butter. Pour over trout and serve.

Makes 4 servings.

Notes:

Curried Scallops and Apple

5 tbsp	**butter**	*75 mL*
1	**Apple, peeled, cored, chopped**	*1*
1/2	**onion, chopped**	*1/2*
1 tbsp	**all purpose flour**	*15 mL*
1 tsp	**curry powder**	*5 mL*
1/2 cup	**dry white wine**	*125 mL*
1/2 cup	**whipping cream**	*125 mL*
1/2 cup	**chicken stock**	*125 mL*
1 1/2 cups	**chopped tomatoes**	*375 mL*
1/2 tsp	**sugar**	*2 mL*
1	**large garlic clove, chopped fine**	*1*
1 tsp	**chopped fresh basil or 1/2 tsp dried**	*5 mL*
1 tsp	**chopped fresh rosemary or 1/2 tsp dried**	*5 mL*
12	**large fresh sea scallops**	*12*

Melt 1 tbsp butter in medium saucepan over medium heat. Add chopped Apple and onion to pan; sauté until onion is soft and translucent, about 5 minutes. Add flour and curry powder; stir 1 minute. Add wine, cream and stock; stir until mixture thickens to sauce consistency, about 3 minutes. Stir in tomatoes and sugar. Season with salt and pepper.

Meanwhile, prepare barbecue or preheat broiler. Melt remaining 4 tbsp butter in small saucepan over medium heat. Stir in garlic, basil and rosemary. Remove from heat. Brush scallops with melted herb butter. Grill or broil scallops until opaque in center, about 3 minutes per side.

Spoon sauce over scallops and serve.

Makes 4 servings

Sweet and Sour Shrimp and Apples

Shrimp cooks quickly and tastes terrific – prepare all the ingredients before you turn the heat on under the wok – and get cooking!

3 tbsp	**vegetable oil**	*45 mL*
1 lb	**shrimp, peeled and deveined**	*500 g*
2	**Apples, cored and thinly sliced**	*2*
1 cup	**green onion, cut into 1-inch pieces**	*250 mL*
1	**sweet red pepper, cut into strips**	*1*
1 1/2 cups	**fresh snow peas**	*375 mL*
1/2 cup	**cold water**	*125 mL*
1/3 cup	**firmly packed brown sugar**	*75 mL*
1/4 cup	**rice wine or cider vinegar**	*50 mL*
4 tsp	**cornstarch**	*20 mL*
1 tbsp	**reduced-sodium soy sauce**	*15 mL*
1 tsp	**ground ginger**	*5 mL*
	Rice or Chow Mein noodles (optional)	

In large saucepan or wok, heat 1 tbsp oil over high heat; stir fry shrimp until just pink. Transfer shrimp to bowl and reserve. Add another tbsp oil to saucepan; add Apples and stir-fry 1 minute. Transfer to bowl with shrimp. Add remaining tbsp oil to saucepan; add green onion, sweet pepper, and snow peas; stir-fry 2 minutes. Transfer vegetables to bowl with shrimp.

In small bowl, combine water, brown sugar, vinegar, cornstarch, soy sauce, and ginger; mix until well-blended. Pour mixture into saucepan and cook, stirring constantly, until boiling and thickened. Reduce heat to low, return all ingredients to saucepan and heat through. Serve with rice or noodles, if desired.

Makes 4 servings.

When cooking with Apples, choose from:

Empire

Northern Spy

Spartan

Golden Delicious

Creamy Pork & Apples with Cornmeal-Yogurt Biscuits

1	**small onion finely chopped**	*1*
3	**garlic cloves minced**	*3*
2	**Apples, peeled cored and sliced**	*2*
2 tsp	**sugar**	*10 mL*
2 tsp	**dry sage**	*10 mL*
1/4 tsp	**white pepper**	*1 mL*
1/4 tsp	**ground nutmeg**	*1 mL*
2 1/2	**pounds pork, boneless fresh leg trimmed & cut into 1" cubes**	*1.25 kg*
3 tbsp	**flour**	*45 mL*
1/2 cup	**dry white wine**	*125 mL*
1 1/2 tbsp	**cornstarch**	*22 mL*
1/3 cup	**whipping cream**	*75 mL*

Cornmeal Yogurt Biscuits:

1 1/2 cups	**flour**	*375 mL*
1/2 cup	**yellow cornmeal**	*125 mL*
1 tbsp	**baking powder**	*15 mL*
1 tsp	**sugar**	*5 mL*
1/2 tsp	**salt**	*2 mL*
1/3 cup	**cold butter/margarine**	*75 mL*
3/4 cup	**plain yogurt**	*175 mL*

Combine onion, garlic, and Apples; sprinkle with sugar, sage, white pepper, and nutmeg. Coat pork cubes with flour, then arrange over Apple mixture (in crockpot). Pour in wine. Cover and cook LOW until pork very tender. When pork is almost done, prepare biscuits.

Biscuits:
In a large bowl, mix flour, cornmeal, baking powder, sugar and salt. Cut in butter. Add yogurt, stir just to form sticky ball. Gather ball

and knead slightly on floured board. Roll or pat out about 1/2" thick. Using a 2 1/2" cutter, cut 12 rounds. Place about 1" apart on an ungreased baking sheet. Bake at 450 degrees F until golden brown.

While biscuits are baking, mix cornstarch and cream in a small bowl; blend into pork mixture. Increase cooker heat setting to HIGH; cover and cook until sauce is hot and bubbly (10-15 minutes). Season to taste. Arrange 6 biscuits around pork mixture in cooker. Serve remaining biscuits hot in a basket.

Makes 6 servings

Apple-Glazed Roast Pork - Crockpot

Slow cooking is simplicity itself.

4 lbs	**trimmed pork loin roast**	***2 kg***
	salt & pepper to taste	
6	**Apples, peeled, cored and quartered**	***6***
1/4 cup	**pure Apple juice**	***50 mL***
3 tbsp	**brown sugar**	***45 mL***
1 tsp	**ground ginger**	***5 mL***

Rub roast with salt and pepper. Brown pork roast under broiler to remove excess fat; drain well. Place Apple quarters in bottom of crockpot. Place roast on top of Apples. Combine Apple juice, brown sugar, and ginger. Spoon over top surface of roast, moistening well. Cover and cook on Low setting for 10 to 12 hours or until done.

Makes 8 servings.

Grilled Pork Tenderloin in a Mustard, Rosemary & Apple Marinade

1/4 cup	**pure Apple juice**	*50 mL*
1/4 cup	**Dijon mustard**	*50 mL*
2 tbsp	**olive oil**	*25 mL*
2 tbsp	**chopped fresh rosemary**	*25 mL*
4	**cloves garlic, minced**	*4*
1 tsp	**crushed black peppercorns**	*5 mL*
2 3/4 pound	**pork tenderloins, trimmed of fat**	*1.75 kg*
1 tbsp	**minced shallots (1 small shallot)**	*15 mL*
1/4 cup	**port wine**	*50 mL*
2 tbsp	**balsamic vinegar**	*25 mL*
	salt & freshly ground black pepper to taste	
	rosemary sprigs for garnish	

In a small bowl, whisk together Apple juice, 2 tbsp of the mustard, 1 tbsp of the oil, rosemary, garlic and peppercorns. Measure out 3 tbsp and reserve for basting. Place tenderloins in a shallow glass dish and pour the remaining marinade over them, turning to coat. Cover and marinate in the refrigerator for up to 2 hours, turning several times.

In a small bowl or a jar with a tight-fitting lid, combine shallots, port, vinegar, salt, pepper and the remaining 1 1/2 tsp mustard and 1 tbsp olive oil; whisk or shake until blended. Set aside.

Grill the tenderloins, covered, turning several times and basting the browned sides with the reserved marinade, 12 to 16 minutes. Transfer the tenderloins to a clean cutting board and let rest for about 5 minutes before carving into 1/2 inch thick slices. Arrange the pork slices on plates, drizzle with the vinaigrette and garnish plates with rosemary sprigs.

Makes 8 servings.

Apple Cider Pork and Vegetables

If you don't have a crock pot or slow-cooker, use a covered pot in a 225 degree F oven.

2	**small sweet potatoes peel, 1/2" slice**	*2*
2	**Apples, peeled cored and chopped**	*2*
1	**onion sliced thin**	*1*
1	**bay leaf**	*1*
3/4 tsp	**salt**	*3 mL*
1/2 tsp	**pepper**	*2 mL*
1/2 tsp	**dried rosemary crushed**	*2 mL*
1 1/2 lb	**lean boneless pork cut into 1" cubes**	*750 g*
1/2 cup	**all-purpose flour**	*125 mL*
2 tbsp	**canola oil**	*25 mL*
1 cup	**Apple cider**	*250 mL*

Place first 7 ingredients in slow cooker; set aside. Dredge pork in flour and brown in hot oil. Remove pork, reserving drippings in saucepan. Place pork in cooker. Add cider to saucepan, stirring to deglaze; pour over pork. Cover and cook on LOW 6 to 8 hours. Discard bay leaf when serving.

Makes 4 servings.

Beef & Lamb

When cooking with Apples, choose from:
Empire
Northern Spy
Spartan
Golden Delicious

Beef Stew with Apple Dumplings

Zena Tully of Etobicoke, Ontario, is the inspiration behind this recipe.

5 lbs	**stew beef cut into 1 1/2" cubes**	*2.5 kg*
1/2 cup	**flour**	*125 mL*
3	**beef bouillon cubes crushed**	*3*
1/2 tsp	**pepper**	*2 mL*
2 cups	**onions, sliced**	*500 mL*
2	**garlic cloves, minced**	*2*
1/2 cup	**beef broth**	*125 mL*
3/4 cup	**pure Apple juice**	*175 mL*
2 tbsp	**vinegar**	*25 mL*
1 tsp	**thyme**	*5 mL*
1 tsp	**curry**	*5 mL*

Dumplings:

1 cup	**Applesauce**	*250 mL*
2	**eggs, well beaten**	*2*
2 tsp	**parsley, chopped**	*10mL*
2 cups	**flour**	*500 mL*
2 tsp	**baking powder**	*10 mL*
1 tsp	**salt**	*5 mL*

Coat meat with mixture of flour, crushed bouillon and pepper. Combine meat, onion, garlic, beef broth, Apple juice, vinegar, thyme and curry in slow cooker. Cover and cook on auto 7 hours; or high 4 to 5 hours; or low 8 to 10 hours. Remove cover and place tablespoons full of dumpling batter on top of stew. Cover and cook on high for 20 minutes.

To make dumpling batter; blend Applesauce with eggs and parsley; add flour, baking powder and salt and beat into egg mixture.

Makes 8 servings.

Lamb Curry With Apples

1 tsp	**cumin seeds**	*5 mL*
1 tsp	**coriander seeds**	*5 mL*
1 tbsp	**yellow mustard seeds**	*15 mL*
3	**Apples**	*3*
2 tsp	**canola oil**	*10 mL*
2	**large onions, finely chopped**	*2*
6	**cloves garlic, minced**	*6*
1	**jalapeno pepper, seeded and minced**	*1*
2 tbsp	**curry powder**	*25 mL*
1 tsp	**paprika**	*5 mL*
1/2 tsp	**ground cinnamon**	*2 mL*
1 3/4 cup	**beef stock**	*425 mL*
1 lb	**cooked lamb meat, cut into cubes**	*500 g*
1/2 cup	**golden raisins (optional)**	*125 mL*
2 tbsp	**slivered crystallized ginger**	*25 mL*
	salt & freshly ground black pepper to taste	

In a saucepan over medium heat, toast cumin and coriander seeds, stirring about 1 minute. Transfer to a mortar and pestle, grind to a powder; set aside. In the same saucepan, toast mustard seeds until they start to pop, about 1 minute; set aside.

Peel, core and chop 1 Apple. Heat oil in a Dutch oven over medium heat. Add onions and chopped Apple; sauté until softened and golden, 5 to 7 minutes. Add garlic, jalapeno peppers, curry powder, paprika, cinnamon, the reserved mustard seeds and 1 tsp of the ground cumin-coriander mixture; sauté about 2 minutes.

Add beef stock, lamb, raisins and crystallized ginger; bring to a simmer. Cover and cook over low heat for 15 minutes. Peel, core and cut the remaining 2 Apples into 1/2-inch chunks; add them to the lamb mixture and simmer until the lamb is tender and the Apples are soft, about 10 minutes longer. Stir in the remaining ground cumin-coriander mixture. Season with salt and pepper and serve over rice.

Desserts

When a sauce texture is required, choose from:
Cortland
Empire
McIntosh
Golden Delicious
Russet
Northern Spy

When a firmer, 'pie' texture is required, choose from:
Cortland
Spartan
Idared
Crispin (Mutsu)
McIntosh
Russet
Northern Spy
Golden Delicious

Candy Apples

8	**wooden ice cream sticks**	***8***
8	**Apples**	***8***
1 cup	**water**	***250 mL***
3 cups	**sugar**	***750 mL***
1/2 cup	**light corn syrup**	***125 mL***
1/4 cup	**red hot candies**	***50 mL***
1/2 tsp	**red food colour**	***2 mL***

Wash and dry apples. Insert wooden sticks part way into the stem-end of the Apples. Grease a large cookie sheet.

In a large saucepan combine all remaining ingredients and heat to boiling without stirring. Boil until candy thermometer reads 290 degrees F, or until the mixture reaches the hard ball stage (about 20 minutes). You can test this by dropping a little of the mixture into cold water, it should separate and form thin hard threads.

Remove syrup from heat. Swirl each Apple into the mixture to coat. Place Apples on cookie sheet to cool. Resoften syrup over low heat if necessary. Chill for at least an hour.

Notes:

Apple Roll

2 cups	**flour**	***500 mL***
1 pinch	**salt**	***pinch***
2 tbsp	**shortening**	***25 mL***
1/2 cup	**milk**	***125 mL***
2 tsp	**baking powder**	***10 mL***
2 tbsp	**sugar**	***25 mL***
2-3	**Apples, peeled, cored and chopped**	***2-3***
1 1/2 cups	**sugar**	***375 mL***
2 cups	**water**	***500 mL***
	additional sugar	
	butter	
	cinnamon	

Mix together flour, salt, shortening, milk, baking powder and 2 tbsp sugar. Roll dough an inch thick, spread with chopped Apples.

Roll up and cut into 1 1/2-inch slices. Combine 1/2 cups sugar and water in a pan and heat to boiling. Place rolls in baking pan of hot syrup. Sprinkle with sugar, cinnamon and butter and bake at 350 degrees F until brown.

Notes:

Allspice Apple Cake With Happy Apple Sauce

Sauce:

1 cup	**pure Apple juice**	***250 mL***
1 cup	**whipping cream**	***250 mL***
1 cup	**packed golden brown sugar**	***250 mL***
1/4 cup	**unsalted butter**	***50 mL***
1 3/4 tsp	**ground allspice**	***8 mL***
1/4 tsp	**cider vinegar**	***1 mL***

Cake:

2 cups	**plus 2 tbsp all purpose flour**	***500 mL***
1 tbsp	**ground allspice**	***15 mL***
1 1/2 tsp	**ground cinnamon**	***7 mL***
1 1/2 tsp	**baking powder**	***7 mL***
1 tsp	**baking soda**	***5 mL***
3/4 tsp	**salt**	***3 mL***
1/4 tsp	**ground cloves**	***1 mL***
4	**large eggs**	***4***
1 1/4 cups	**sugar**	***310 mL***
1 cup	**packed golden brown sugar**	***250 mL***
3/4 cup	**vegetable oil**	***175 mL***
1 tbsp	**fresh lemon juice**	***15 mL***
1 1/2 lbs	**Apples, peeled, cored, cubed**	***750 g***
1 cup	**coarsely chopped toasted walnuts**	***250 mL***
	Vanilla ice cream	

Sauce: Bring first 5 ingredients to boil in heavy medium saucepan over high heat, stirring until sugar dissolves. Boil gently until sauce thickens and coats spoon thickly, stirring occasionally, about

25 minutes. Add vinegar. Rewarm before using.

Preheat oven to 350 degrees F. Butter and flour 9xl3-inch pan with 2- inch-high sides. Combine 2 cups flour with next 6 ingredients in medium bowl and reserve.

In another bowl and using an electric mixer, beat eggs, 1 1/4 cups sugar, 1 cup brown sugar, oil and lemon juice until very thick, about 4 minutes. Mix in flour mixture. Toss Apples and walnuts with 2 tbsp flour. Add to batter. Transfer to prepared pan. Bake until tester inserted into centre of cake comes out clean, about 1 hour 5 minutes.

While cake is still hot, pour 1/2 cup sauce over cake, spreading evenly. Cool cake in pan at least 1 hour. Cut cake into squares. Top with ice cream. Spoon remaining warm sauce over.

Makes 12 generous servings.

Notes:

Apple Ice

In Italy, this refreshing naturally-flavoured ice is called granita. It is best served after a rich meal or in the middle of a hot day.

5 cups	**Apples peeled and sliced**	***1.25 L***
1 cup	**water**	***250 mL***
3/4 cup	**sugar**	***175 mL***
1/2 tsp	**finely grated lemon zest**	***2 mL***

In large pot, simmer apples, water, and sugar until Apples are tender, about 20 minutes. In food processor or blender, purée mixture until smooth; stir in lemon zest. Transfer mixture to 8 or 9-inch metal pan and freeze until solid. Return to food processor of blender and purée until chunks break up and mixture is fluffy. Refreeze until firm.

Makes 8 servings.

Notes:

Apple-Layered Pound Cake

Sylvia Agnes McClory inspired this cake, this cook and this loving memory.

2 lbs	**Apples, peeled, cored and thinly sliced**	*1 kg*
5 tbsp	**sugar**	*75 mL*
2 tbsp	**cinnamon**	*25 mL*
3 cups	**all purpose flour**	*750 mL*
2-1/2 cups	**sugar**	*675 mL*
1 cup	**vegetable oil**	*250 mL*
4	**eggs**	*4*
1/4 cup	**fresh orange juice**	*50 mL*
1 tbsp	**baking powder**	*15 mL*
2-1/2 tsp	**vanilla**	*12 mL*
1/2 tsp	**salt**	*2 mL*
	powder sugar	

Preheat oven to 350 degrees F. Grease 10 inch tube pan. Combine Apples, sugar and cinnamon; set aside.

In large bowl of electric mixer, combine flour, sugar, oil, eggs, juice, baking powder, vanilla and salt. Beat until thoroughly mixed (batter will be heavy). Spoon half of batter into prepared pan. Top with half of Apples. Repeat with remaining batter and Apples. Bake until top of cake is brown and firm to touch, about 1-3/4 hours.

Cool cake 1-1/2 hours. Remove from pan. Sprinkle with powdered sugar. Serve warm.

Applesauce Spice Cake

A wonderful, moist cake. Serve Sunday morning with coffee.

2 cups	**flour**	***500 mL***
2 tsp	**ground cinnamon**	***10 mL***
2 tsp	**baking powder**	***10 mL***
1/2 tsp	**salt**	***2 mL***
1 tsp	**allspice**	***5 mL***
1/2 tsp	**mace**	***2 mL***
1 cup	**chopped walnuts**	***250 mL***
1 cup	**raisins (optional)**	***250 mL***
1/2 cup	**unsalted butter, softened**	***125 mL***
1/2 cup	**maple syrup**	***125 mL***
1/2 cup	**brown sugar**	***125 mL***
1 tsp	**vanilla**	***5 mL***
2 cups	**Applesauce**	***500 mL***

Preheat oven to 350 degrees F. Mix all dry ingredients together. Cream softened butter with maple syrup, sugar and vanilla. Add Applesauce and mix well. Add to dry ingredients a little at a time. Beat well. Spoon into a buttered cake pan and bake 45 minutes to 1 hour at 350 degrees F. Cake is done when wooden toothpick inserted into centre comes out clean.

Notes:

Crispy Apple Turnovers

This is a great recipe to take advantage of the many varieties of Apples available in the autumn months.

Filling Ingredients:

6	**Apples, peeled, cored and diced**	***6***
2 tbsp	**brown sugar**	***25 mL***
1 tsp	**cinnamon**	***5 mL***
2 tbsp	**butter**	***25 mL***

Pastry Ingredients:

2 cups	**flour**	***250 mL***
3/4 cup	**butter, very cold**	***175 mL***
1/2 cup	**ice water**	***125 mL***
1	**egg, beaten with a little water**	***1***

Place flour in a mixing bowl. Using two butter knives, cut butter into flour until it resembles coarse meal. Sprinkle ice water over flour mixture and mix until dough forms. Knead dough lightly, wrap in plastic and place in refrigerator until needed.

In a saucepan, melt butter and sauté apples for about a minute until soft. Add brown sugar and cinnamon and toss to coat Apples. Let cool. Sprinkle some flour on a pastry board or counter top and roll out dough to a 1/4" thickness. Cut out 6" squares. Put some of the Apple mixture on top of each square. Fold over to form a triangle and press the edges down with a fork to seal. (Make sure you vent each turnover by making some fork pricks in the top.)

Brush egg wash on top of each triangle sparingly and sprinkle lightly with some brown sugar. Place turnovers on a greased cookie sheet and bake at 350 degrees F for 10 minutes or until golden brown.

Apple Temptation

2 1/2 lbs	**Apples, peeled and cored**	***1.25 kg***
1/2 cup	**butter, melted**	***125 mL***
2/3 cup	**flour**	***150 mL***
1/2 cup	**sugar**	***125 mL***
1 1/4 cups	**milk**	***300 mL***
4	**eggs**	***4***
1 tbsp	**vanilla**	***15 mL***
2 tsp	**baking powder**	***10 mL***
1/2 tsp	**salt**	***2 mL***
	additional sugar	
	whipped cream	

Dice Apples and place in buttered, floured 2-quart rectangular baking dish. In a blender, combine butter, flour, sugar, milk, eggs, vanilla, baking powder and salt. Blend until evenly combined.

Pour mixture over Apples and bake at 400 degrees F 35 to 40 minutes, or until set in centre. Serve at once, sprinkled with sugar and accompanied by whipped cream.

Notes:

Mulled Apple Cider Sorbet

In Ontario, fresh cider is found at roadside stands, farmers markets and supermarkets in the fall and winter.

6 cups	**Apple cider**	*1.5 L*
3-inch	**cinnamon stick**	*7.5 cm*
1/2 cup	**sugar**	*125 mL*
2 tsp	**strained fresh lemon juice**	*10 mL*

In a large saucepan combine the cider, the cinnamon stick, the sugar, and a pinch of salt and boil the mixture for 5 to 10 minutes, or until the liquid is reduced to about 4 cups. Stir in the lemon juice, strain the mixture through a fine sieve into a bowl, and chill it, covered, until it is cold. Freeze the mixture in an ice cream freezer according to the manufacturer's instructions.

Makes about 1 1/4 quarts.

Notes:

Apple Roly-Poly

Cindy Savage, with her stories of summer camp and startling culinary skills, inspired this dessert.

1 cup	**Apple cider**	***250 mL***
1/2 cup	**light brown sugar**	***125 mL***
2 tbsp	**fresh lemon juice**	***25 mL***
2	**Apples, peeled and grated**	***2***
1/4 cup	**currants (optional)**	***50 mL***
1/4 tsp	**ground cinnamon**	***1 mL***
1/4 tsp	**ground allspice**	***1 mL***
1 cup	**all-purpose white flour**	***250 mL***
1-1/2 tsp	**baking powder**	***7 mL***
1/2 tsp	**baking soda**	***2 mL***
1/2 tsp	**ground ginger**	***2 mL***
1/8 tsp	**salt**	***.5 mL***
2 tbsp	**cold butter, cut into pieces**	***25 mL***
1/2 cup	**buttermilk**	***125 mL***

Preheat oven to 375 degrees F. In a small bowl, stir together cider, brown sugar and 1 tbsp of the lemon juice; pour the mixture into four 12-oz custard cups. Set the cups on a baking sheet and place them in the oven to heat the syrup while you prepare the filling and dough.

To make filling: Combine Apples, currants, cinnamon, allspice and the remaining 1 tbsp lemon juice. Set aside.

To make the biscuit dough: Whisk together flour, baking powder, baking soda, ginger and salt in a bowl. Cut butter into the dry ingredients with two forks until the mixture resembles coarse meal. With a fork, gradually stir in just enough of the buttermilk to make a soft dough.

On a well-floured surface, pat the dough into an 8-inch square. Distribute the grated-Apple mixture evenly over the surface. Roll up the dough and filling like a jelly roll. Slice the roll into 4 pieces. Carefully remove the syrup-filled cups from the oven. Place a roly-poly piece cut-side down in each cup, pressing on the dough to flatten slightly. (As the roly-polys bake, they expand to fill the dishes and absorb most of the syrup.) Bake for 15 to 20 minutes, or until the dough is baked through to the centre.

Serve immediately.

Eve's Apple

1	**Apple**	***1***
1 tbsp	**raisins**	***15 mL***
1 1/2 tsp	**brown sugar**	***7 mL***
1/4 tsp	**cinnamon**	***1 mL***
2 tbsp	**sour cream**	***25 mL***

Core Apple almost to, but not through, bottom. Mix together raisins, brown sugar and cinnamon. Stuff Apple cavity. Cover with plastic wrap. Pierce plastic to allow for steam. Microwave on HIGH (100% power) 2 to 3 minutes. Test with skewer. (Apple will continue to cook on standing.) Let stand several minutes or until cool. Serve with sour cream if desired.

Makes 1 serving.

Apple Rhubarb Crisp

The eggs make a big difference to this old standby.

Apple Filling		
2 cups	**Apples peeled and finely sliced**	***500 mL***
2 cups	**rhubarb, finely cut**	***500mL***
2	**eggs, separated**	***2***
1 cup	**white sugar**	***250 mL***
2 tbsp	**all purpose flour**	***25 mL***
1/2 tsp	**salt**	***2 mL***
Topping:		***125 mL***
1/2 cup	**white sugar**	***125 mL***
1/2 cup	**all purpose flour**	***5 mL***
1 tsp	**cinnamon**	***1 mL***
1/4 tsp	**nutmeg**	***125 mL***
1/2 cup	**butter**	***125 mL***
1/2 cup	**chopped nuts**	

Filling: Place finely cut fruits in a bowl and set aside. Sift sugar, flour and salt together. Finely sift this mixture into fruits, turning frequently. Beat egg yolks and stir into floured mixture. Beat egg whites until stiff and fold gently into fruit mixture. Transfer to buttered casserole (9 X 9" pan).

Topping: Sift flour, sugar, cinnamon and nutmeg together, then crumble the butter into the dry ingredients. When well-mixed, but still grainy, add chopped nuts and mix lightly. Sprinkle topping over Apple-rhubarb mixture, covering well.

Bake 375 degree F oven for 30 - 40 minutes or until fruit is tender.

Apple Drop Cookies

1/2 cup	**soft shortening**	*125 mL*
1 1/3 cups	**brown sugar**	*325 mL*
1/2 tsp	**salt**	*2 mL*
1 tsp	**cinnamon**	*5 mL*
1 tsp	**ground cloves**	*5 mL*
1/2 tsp	**nutmeg**	*2 mL*
1	**egg**	*1*
2 cups	**flour**	*500 mL*
1 tsp	**baking soda**	*5 mL*
1/4 cup	**pure Apple juice or milk**	*50 mL*
1 cup	**chopped nuts**	*250 mL*
1 cup	**Apples finely chopped**	*250 mL*
1 cup	**raisins (optional)**	*250 mL*

FROSTING: Combine all ingredients to good spreading consistency.

1 1/2 cups	**icing sugar**	*375 mL*
1 tbsp	**melted butter**	*15 mL*
1/2 tsp	**vanilla**	*2 mL*
1/8 tsp	**salt**	*.5 mL*
2 1/2 tbsp	**light cream.**	*35 mL*

Preheat oven to 375 degrees F. In mixing bowl combine shortening, sugar, salt, spices and egg. Beat well. Sift together flour and baking soda and add to bowl. Stir in Apple juice. Add nuts, raisins and Apples.

Drop batter by tablespoon onto greased cookie sheets. Bake 11 to 14 minutes until light brown. Spread while hot with frosting.

Makes 48 cookies.

Apple Praline Cheesecake

Erin Stockman of Kingston, Ontario, inspired this recipe. Her tradition of bringing cheesecake in to work for the staff at Christmas is a delightfully anticipated event.

Crust:

1 cup	**Graham cracker crumbs**	***250 mL***
2 tbsp	**sugar**	***25 mL***
2 tbsp	**butter**	***25 mL***

Apple Mix:

1/4 cup	**butter**	***50 mL***
1/2 cup	**light brown sugar**	***125 mL***
2 lbs	**Apple peeled, cored, dice**	***1 kg***
1 tsp	**cinnamon**	***5 mL***
1/2 tsp	**nutmeg**	***2 mL***
1/2 tsp	**allspice**	***2 mL***

Praline Topping:

1 1/2 cups	**dark brown sugar**	***375 mL***
1/2 cup	**butter, softened**	***125 mL***
1 cup	**pecan pieces**	***250 mL***

Apple Cheesecake:

16 oz	**cream cheese softened**	***500 mL***
1/2 cup	**granulated sugar**	***125 mL***
3 large	**eggs**	***3***
1 cup	**heavy whipping cream**	***250 mL***

Crust: Melt butter. Stir in the crumbs and sugar until thoroughly blended. Press into the bottom of a 9" springform pan. Set aside.

Apple Mix: In a Dutch oven, melt butter over low heat, add brown sugar, apples, cinnamon, nutmeg and allspice. Simmer over low heat until apples are soft, but still hold their shape. Cool mixture to room temperature and reserve.

Praline Topping: In a small bowl, mix brown sugar, and pecan pieces together with a fork until well incorporated. Reserve.

Cheesecake: In a large bowl with an electric mixer cream together sugar and cream cheese on medium speed until light and fluffy. Beat in the eggs one at a time until smooth. Add the cream and continue beating until the mixture is thick and creamy. Gently stir in the cooled apple mix by hand.

Pour into the prepared spring form pan. Spread praline topping over the top. Bake at 350 degrees F for 1 hour and 20 minutes. Allow to cool to room temperature before removing the sides of the pan. Refrigerate until ready to serve. Garnish with whipped cream.

Notes:

Caramelized Apple Parfaits

Creativity counts, think about the wonderful ice-cream sundaes, put out small dishes of candy sprinkles, chocolate chips, maraschino cherries, whipped cream and get surreal!

2 cups	**plain yogurt**	***500 mL***
2/3 cup	**sugar**	***150 mL***
2 tsp	**butter**	***10 mL***
4	**Apples peeled, cored and thinly sliced**	***4***
1 tbsp	**fresh lemon juice**	***15 mL***
1 tbsp	**chopped toasted walnuts (optional)**	***15 mL***

Draining the yogurt for half an hour gives it enough body so it can be layered in a parfait glass with the cooked Apples. Line a colander or sieve with cheesecloth or a coffee filter and set it over a bowl. Spoon in yogurt and let drain for about 30 minutes.

Meanwhile, in a medium-size heavy saucepan, stir together sugar and 2 tbsp water. Bring to a boil, stirring to dissolve the sugar. Cook, without stirring, until the syrup turns deep amber, about 5 minutes. (Do not let the syrup burn.) Remove the pan from the heat, add butter and swirl the pan until butter has melted. Add Apples and lemon juice. Return to low heat, cover and cook for 5 minutes. Uncover, and cook, stirring occasionally, until Apples are tender and translucent and the juice has thickened slightly, 15 to 20 minutes. Let cool slightly, about 5 minutes.

Spoon alternating layers of the caramelized Apples and drained yogurt into 4 parfait or wineglasses. Sprinkle walnuts over top, if desired.

Candy Apple Cheesecake Pie

If you have fond memories of that one house on the block with caramel Apples on a stick at Hallowe'en, the flavours and textures of this dessert will take you back in time.

Filling:

2 tbsp	**butter or margarine**	***25 mL***
1/2 cups	**firmly packed brown sugar**	***125 mL***
4	**Apples, peeled, cored, sliced thinly**	***4***
21	**caramels, unwrapped**	***21***
1/4 cups	**half and half**	***50 mL***
1-8oz	**pkg. of cream cheese**	***250 mL***
1/2 cup	**firmly packed brown sugar**	***125 mL***
1/2 tsp	**allspice**	***2 mL***
1 1/2 tsp	**vanilla extract**	***7 mL***
1	**egg**	***1***
	One frozen pie crust	

Topping:

1/2 cup	**small chocolate chips**	***125 mL***
3/4 cup	**pecans or walnuts, chopped finely**	***175 mL***
	Whip cream	

In a large saucepan, melt butter and 1/2 cup brown sugar; stirring constantly. Add Apples; cook and stir 12-15 minutes until Apples are golden and tender. Set aside. Drain if necessary. In top of double-boiler or heavy saucepan, melt caramels with half and half until mixture is smooth, stirring frequently. Keep warm!

In a small bowl, beat cream cheese and 1/2 cup brown sugar until light and fluffy. Add 1/2 tsp allspice, vanilla, and egg; beat until blended.

Heat oven to 350 degrees F. Fold half of caramel mixture into cream cheese mixture, and the other half of caramel mixture into the Apples. Mix Well. Spoon Apple mixture into cooled pie crust. In a small bowl, combine topping ingredients; reserve 2 tbsp mixture. Sprinkle remaining mixture on top of Apple mixture in pie crust. Top with caramel cream cheese mixture.

Bake at 350 degrees F for 30-40 minutes until deep golden or until pie is set. Cool completely. Garnish with whip cream, chocolate chips and nuts.

Apple Brown Betty

2 cups	**soft bread crumbs**	***500 mL***
1/4 cup	**butter**	***50 mL***
3 cups	**Apples, cored and sliced**	***750 mL***
1/2 cup	**sugar**	***125 mL***
1 tsp	**cinnamon**	***5 mL***
3/4 cup	**water**	***175 mL***

Sauté bread crumbs in butter. Add Apples, sugar, cinnamon, and water. If saucepan is oven-proof, cover and place in oven. Otherwise transfer to greased baking dish. Bake at 375 degrees F for 30 - 40 minutes or until Apples are tender. Add water if Apples appear to be drying out during baking.

Serve with vanilla ice cream.

Makes 4 servings.

Apple Dumplings

For an extra special sweet surprise, spoon raisins, dried cranberries, or dried cherries into the centre of each Apple before wrapping it with pastry.

Syrup

1 2/3 cups	**water**	*150 mL*
1/2 cup	**sugar**	*125 mL*
1/4 tsp	**ground nutmeg**	*1 mL*
1/4 tsp	**ground cinnamon**	*1 mL*
	Few drops red food colouring (optional)	
1 tbsp	**margarine or butter**	*15 mL*

Dumplings

	Pastry for double-crust pie	
4	**Apples, peeled and cored**	*4*
2 tbsp	**sugar**	*25 mL*
1/8 tsp	**ground nutmeg**	*.5 mL*
1/8 tsp	**ground cinnamon**	*.5 mL*
	Ice cream (optional)	

For syrup, in a medium saucepan combine water, sugar, nutmeg, cinnamon and, if desired, food colouring. Bring to boiling. Reduce heat and simmer, uncovered, for 5 minutes. Remove from heat; stir in margarine or butter.

For dumplings, prepare pastry as directed (see page 180), except divide dough into 4 equal portions. Form each into a ball. On a lightly floured surface, roll each portion of dough into a circle about 1/8 inch thick. Trim each portion to an 8-inch circle. Place 1 Apple in centre of each pastry circle. Combine the sugar, nutmeg, and cinnamon; sprinkle over fruit. Moisten edge of pastry with water. Bring dough up around Apple to resemble a bundle, pressing the edges together at the top to seal. Using a knife or small cookie cutter, cut leaf shapes from pastry scraps. Moisten bottom sides of pastry leaves with water and place leaves on top of the wrapped Apples, gently pressing to seal. Place wrapped Apples in an ungreased 2-quart square baking dish. Pour syrup over dumplings. Bake in a preheated 375 degrees F oven about 45 minutes, or till Apples are tender and pastry is golden. Serve warm with ice cream, if desired.

Apple Dabble Cake

This recipe is a favourite among the folks at Creasy Apple Dabble Farm located in Prince Edward County.

2 cups	**sugar**	***500 mL***
1 cup	**vegetable oil**	***250 mL***
3	**eggs**	***3***
2 tsp	**vanilla**	***10 mL***
3 cups	**flour**	***750 mL***
1 tsp	**salt**	***5 mL***
1 tsp	**baking soda**	***5 mL***
2 tsp	**cinnamon**	***10 mL***
4 cups	**Apples, cored, peeled and chopped**	***1 L***

Mix ingredients by hand in order given. Pour into 13"x9" pan. Bake at 350 degrees F for 30-40 minutes.

Meanwhile in saucepan, combine 1 cup brown sugar, 1/4 cup cream or milk, 1/4 lb butter. Boil 4 minutes. Pour over baked cake and return to oven for a few minutes before serving.

Creamy Apple Crisp

3 cups	**Apples sliced, peeled**	***750 mL***
3 oz	**pkg Cream Cheese**	***100 g***
3/4 cup	**sour cream**	***175 mL***
3/4 cup	**sugar**	***175 mL***
1	**egg**	***1***
1/2 tsp	**vanilla**	***2 mL***
1/4 cup	**butter, room temperature**	***50 mL***
1/4 cup	**quick cooking oatmeal**	***50 mL***
1/4 cup	**all-purpose flour**	***50 mL***
1/4 cup	**brown sugar**	***50 mL***
1/4 cup	**granulated sugar**	***50 mL***
1 tsp	**cinnamon**	***5 mL***

Put Apples in a 2 quart casserole dish. Beat cream cheese, sour cream, sugar, egg, and vanilla until light. Stir mixture into Apples. For topping: cut butter into oatmeal, flour, sugars and cinnamon. Sprinkle on top of Apples.

Bake at 350 degrees F for 35 - 40 minutes or until golden brown.

Notes:

Apple Crisp

This is a 'back to basics' recipe an awful lot of highly-respected, old-fashioned politicians believe is the best. But don't expect them to bake it!

4 cups	**Apples, peeled cored and sliced**	***1 L***
1/4 cup	**water**	***50 mL***

Topping (blend together):

3/4 cup	**flour**	***175 mL***
1/2 tsp	**salt**	***2 mL***
1 cup	**sugar**	***250 mL***
1/3 cup	**butter**	***75 mL***
1 tsp	**cinnamon**	***5 mL***

Place Apples in a shallow baking dish. Sprinkle water over the Apples. Spread crumb mixture over Apples. Bake uncovered about 40 minutes in moderate oven, 350 degrees F. Serve warm with whipped cream or ice cream.

Makes 6 servings.

Notes:

Applesauce Apple Crisp

3 cups	**Apples sliced**	***750 mL***
16 oz	**Applesauce**	***500 mL***
1/2 cup	**raisins**	***125 mL***
1/2 cup	**sugar**	***125 mL***
1 tsp	**cinnamon**	***5 mL***
1 tsp	**nutmeg**	***5 mL***
1/2 tsp	**salt**	***2 mL***
1 cup	**brown sugar**	***250 mL***
3/4 cup	**rolled oats**	***175 mL***
3/4 cup	**flour**	***175 mL***
1/2 cup	**margarine, softened**	***125 mL***

Combine Apples, Applesauce, raisins, sugar and spices. Place in 1 quart baking dish. For topping, mix brown sugar, oats, flour, and margarine until crumbly. Sprinkle over Apple mixture and bake at 350 degrees F for 35 minutes.

Makes 8 servings.

Notes:

Cranberry Apple Crunch

Mark Gardiner of Prince Edward County, says this recipe is so easy that even he can make it. But he usually asks his wife, Betty, to do it for him instead.

1 cup	**sugar**	***250 mL***
1 cup	**water**	***250 mL***
2 cups	**cranberries**	***500 mL***
2 cups	**Apples, peeled, cored and chopped**	***500 mL***
	Crunchy Topping	
	whipped cream	

Mix sugar and water in a saucepan and bring to a boil. Boil for about 5 minutes. Add the cranberries and cook until the skins pop, about 5 minutes. Remove from heat and add Apples. Pour into a buttered 9 x 9" baking dish. Sprinkle with the crumb topping (below). Bake in a 350 degree F oven for about 35 minutes. Cut into 6 to 8 squares and serve warm with whipped cream.

Crunchy Topping: Combine

1/4 cup	**melted butter**	***50 mL***
3/4 cup	**firmly packed brown sugar**	***175 mL***
1 tsp	**ground cinnamon**	***5 mL***
1/2 cup	**walnuts (optional)**	***125 mL***
1/2 cup	**Graham cracker crumbs**	***125 mL***

Makes 6-8 servings.

Graham Apple Coffee Cake

1 cup	**Graham cracker crumbs**	*250 mL*
1 cup	**all-purpose flour**	*250 mL*
1/2 cup	**firmly packed light brown sugar**	*125 mL*
2 tsp	**baking powder**	*10 mL*
1 tsp	**ground cinnamon**	*5 mL*
1/4 tsp	**salt**	*1 mL*
1/3 cup	**margarine, softened**	*75 mL*
1 cup	**milk**	*250 mL*
2	**eggs**	*2*
2 cups	**Apples, peeled, cored & chopped**	*500 mL*
1 cup	**Apple crumb topping (recipe below)**	*250 mL*

In large bowl, combine Graham cracker crumbs, flour, brown sugar, baking powder, cinnamon and salt. Add margarine and milk, with electric mixer at medium speed, beat 2 minutes. Add eggs; beat 2 minutes more. Spread batter in greased 9 x 9″ pan, sprinkle chopped Apple over top. Sprinkle crumb topping (recipe below) evenly over Apples. Bake at 350 degrees F for 35-40 minutes. Serve warm or cold, best when warm!

Crumb Topping: Combine

1/4 cup	**melted margarine**	*50 mL*
3/4 cup	**firmly packed brown sugar**	*175 mL*
1 tsp	**ground cinnamon**	*5 mL*
1/2 cup	**Graham cracker crumbs**	*125 mL*

Makes 9 servings.

Loyalist Apple Cake

After the American Revolution, families loyal to Britain fled America to settle in Canada. This recipe has its roots in the traditions of the United Empire Loyalists who settled, farmed and planted Apple orchards in Upper Canada.

1 1/2 cups	**all-purpose flour**	*375 mL*
2 tsp	**baking powder**	*10 mL*
1/2 tsp	**salt**	*2 mL*
1 cup	**sugar**	*250 mL*
1/4 lb	**butter**	*125 g*
1/2 cup	**milk**	*125 mL*
1	**egg**	*1*
5	**Apples, cut into eighths**	*5*
1/2 tsp	**cinnamon**	*2 mL*
2 tbsp	**raisins (optional)**	*25 mL*
	whipping cream	

Preheat oven to 400 degrees F. Butter and lightly flour a 10 x 6 x 2" baking dish.

Mix the flour, baking powder, salt and 1/2 cup of the sugar together in a large bowl. Melt the butter in a small pan, remove from heat and stir in the milk and the egg, beating well. Add this mixture to the flour mixture and blend well. Pour batter into the prepared pan.

Press the Apple wedges into the batter in uniform rows. Mix the remaining 1/2 cup sugar with the cinnamon and raisins and sprinkle evenly over the top. Bake for 25 minutes or until a toothpick inserted in center comes out clean. Serve with whipped cream.

Apple Crumb Tart

1/2 cup	**butter**	*125 mL*
1/2 cup	**sugar**	*125 mL*
2 cup	**flour**	*500 mL*
1	**egg yolk**	*1*
1 pinch	**baking powder**	*pinch*
1 pinch	**salt**	*pinch*
7	**Apples, peeled & cored**	*7*
1/2 cup	**sugar**	*125 mL*
1/4 cup	**real lemon juice**	*50 mL*
2 cup	**chopped walnuts**	*500 mL*
1/2 cup	**sugar**	*125 mL*
1/2 cup	**brown sugar**	*125 mL*
1/2 tsp	**salt**	*2 mL*
1 1/2 tsp	**cinnamon**	*7 mL*
2/3 cup	**flour**	*150 mL*
1/2 cup	**butter melted**	*125 mL*

Cream butter. Add sugar and egg yolk. Stir in flour and baking powder and a dash of salt, and mix with hands until crumbly. Put into buttered tart pan and bake at 375 degrees F for about 8 minutes or until lightly browned.

Slice Apples, mix with lemon juice and sugar, and microwave covered for about 8 minutes or until tender. Put into crust and bake at 350 degrees F for 15 minutes.

Mix together walnuts, sugar, brown sugar, salt, cinnamon, flour, and melted butter. Spread on top of tart. Return to oven and bake at 350 degrees F for 40 minutes. Serve warm or at room temperature.

Makes 8 servings.

Spiced Cake with Cherry Cream Cheese

2	**eggs**	***2***
1 cup	**vegetable oil**	***250 mL***
1/4 cup	**fresh orange juice**	***50 mL***
2 cups	**sugar**	***500 mL***
2 cups	**all-purpose flour**	***500 mL***
4 tsp	**ground cinnamon**	***20 mL***
1 tsp	**salt**	***5 mL***
2 tsp	**baking soda**	***10 mL***
4 cups	**Apples peeled, cored and chopped**	***1 L***
1 cup	**walnuts, coarsely chopped**	***250 mL***
1/4 cup	**cherry jam**	***50 mL***
1 tbsp	**fresh lime juice**	***15 mL***
2/3 cup	**cream cheese, at room temperature**	***150 mL***

Preheat oven to 325 degrees F. Butter and flour a 10" round cake pan. To make the cake, using an electric mixer set on medium speed, beat the eggs in a large bowl until frothy, 3-4 minutes. Add the vegetable oil and orange juice and mix thoroughly. In a separate bowl, stir together the sugar, flour, cinnamon, salt and baking soda. Add the flour mixture to the egg mixture and beat on low speed until thoroughly combined. Fold in the Apples and walnuts.

Pour the batter into the prepared pan. Bake until firm to the touch and a toothpick inserted into the center comes out clean, about 1 hour; cover the top with aluminum foil if it begins to overbrown. Remove from the oven and let cool in the pan on a rack for 5 minutes, then invert onto the rack. Let cool completely.

Meanwhile, make the cherry cream cheese: In a bowl, combine the jam, lime juice and cream cheese. Using a fork, mash and stir briskly until light and fluffy.To serve, place the cake on a serving plate. Using an icing spatula or knife, spread the cherry cream cheese evenly over the top.

French Apple Tart

This is a classic dessert, simplified by using frozen puff pastry from the supermarket. Brushing the fruit generously with butter before baking will ensure a beautiful golden brown top. Serve warm or at room temperature with cream fraiche or whipped cream, if you like.

	Puff pastry dough	
5	**Apples peeled, cored and thinly sliced**	*5*
2 tbsp	**unsalted butter, melted**	*25 mL*
1 tbsp	**sugar**	*15 mL*

On a lightly floured work surface, roll the dough into a round 12 inches in diameter and 1/8 inch thick. Drape the dough over a rolling pin and transfer it to a 10-inch spring form pan with a removable bottom. Unwrap the dough from the pin and press it gently into the pan. Trim the pastry even with the pan rim and place the pastry-lined pan in the refrigerator.

Preheat an oven to 375 degrees F. Remove the pastry shell from the refrigerator and arrange the Apple slices on top in concentric circles. Brush the Apple slices with the melted butter, coating them evenly, then sprinkle with the sugar. Bake in the oven until golden brown and slightly caramelized, about 50 minutes. If the apples brown too quickly, cover the top loosely with foil. Transfer to a rack and remove the pan sides. Place the tart on a serving plate and serve warm or at room temperature.

Makes 8 servings.

Apple Fritters

Serve hot, with mugs of tea, close your eyes and think of England!

2 tbsp	**sugar**	***25 mL***
2	**eggs**	***2***
1/4 cup	**milk**	***50 mL***
1 cup	**flour**	***250 mL***
2 tsp	**baking powder**	***10 mL***
2 tsp	**lemon juice**	***10 mL***
2 1/2 cups	**Apples sliced**	***625 mL***

Cream together sugar and eggs, add flour and baking powder, then milk. Mix and add lemon juice and Apples. Drop by teaspoonfuls into hot shortening or make into little cakes and fry in a pan like pancakes. Sprinkle powdered sugar and cinnamon over them when finished frying.

Notes:

Apple Gingerbread

Good old fashioned, home spun gingerbread cake. Not likely to run, run, like the gingerbread man!

2-1/2 cups	**flour**	***625 mL***
1 cup	**sugar**	***250 mL***
1 tsp	**baking powder**	***5 mL***
1 tsp	**baking soda**	***5 mL***
1/2 tsp	**salt**	***2 mL***
1 tsp	**cinnamon**	***5 mL***
1 tsp	**ginger**	***5 mL***
1 cup	**molasses**	***250 mL***
1 cup	**buttermilk**	***250 mL***
1/3 cup	**oil**	***75 mL***
2 tsp	**lemon zest**	***10 mL***
1 cup	**Apple (grated with skin)**	***250 mL***
1/2 cup	**raisins, or other dried fruit**	***125 mL***

Mix dry ingredients in a large bowl and add raisins. In another bowl, stir together remaining ingredients. Pour wet ingredients into dry ingredients and mix briefly. Pour into an 8 x 8" pan or a small bundt pan. Bake at 325 degrees F on the lower third of the oven for about an hour.

Notes:

Apple-Raisin Compote

I know we said that raisins were optional in most of these recipes. Here's one where we just couldn't leave them out! The fruit will absorb the liquid as it cooks.

1 1/2 cups	**pure Apple juice**
1/4 tsp	**ground cardamom (or 3 inch stick of cinnamon, broken up)**
4 oz	**dried Apples, chopped**
1/4 cup	**raisins**

In a large 1 quart casserole dish, combine Apple juice and cardamom or cinnamon. Microwave uncovered, on 100% (high) for 3-5 minutes or until boiling. Stir and microwave again on 50% (medium power) for 5 minutes more.

Add Apples and raisins to the hot mixture. Microwave, covered on high for 3-5 minutes or until fruit is softened, stirring once. Remove cinnamon. Serve warm or chilled.

Notes:

Best Pies

The Apple Pie is the best fruit pie in the world. Choose from:

Cortland
Spartan
Idared
Crispin (Mutsu)
McIntosh
Russet
Northern Spy
Golden Delicious

Old Fashioned Dough

Almost all of the pie recipes in this cookbook ask for a frozen pie shell, except for the All-Canada Ten Pound Apple pie on page 184. So if you want to attempt that one, or if you just want your creation to be totally home-made, here is a fool-proof pie crust recipe.

2 1/2 cups	**unbleached all-purpose flour**	***625 mL***
1 tbsp	**sugar**	***15 mL***
1 tsp	**salt**	***5 mL***
8 tbsp	**unsalted butter, chilled and cut into 1 inch pieces for handmixing method, frozen and cut into 1 inch pieces for food processor method**	***100 mL***
1/2 cup	**lard or vegetable shortening, chilled and cut into 1 inch pieces for hand mixing method, frozen and cut into 1 inch pieces for food processor method**	***125 mL***
1	**large egg, beaten**	***1***
1/4 cup	**very cold water (refrigerated or chilled with ice cubes that are removed before measuring)**	***50 mL***

The Hand Method:
In a large bowl, stir together with a wire whisk the flour, sugar, and salt. Add the butter and lard by using your fingertips or a pastry blender, and working them into the flour until the mixture forms pieces the size of peas. (If using vegetable shortening instead of lard, see the variation at the bottom of page 181.)

Combine the beaten egg and cold water. While stirring lightly with a fork, add the egg and water to the flour/fat mixture in a fast, steady stream. Continue stirring, occasionally cleaning off the dough that collects on the tines of the fork, until the flour is almost completely mixed in, but the dough does not form a ball.

Empty the dough onto a flat work surface. Work in the remaining flour by using the heel of your hand to press and push the dough just until it holds together.

Shape the dough into a 6 inch disk. There should be many small pieces of butter and lard visible. Wrap the dough in plastic wrap or wax paper and refrigerate it for at least two hours or overnight.

The Food Processor Method
Measure the flour into the food processor fitted with the steel blade. Add the sugar and salt. Pulse twice to combine.

Add the frozen pieces of butter and lard and process for 8 seconds, until the fat is the size of large peas. (If using vegetable shortening, see the variation below.)

In a liquid measuring cup, combine the beaten egg and cold water. Turn on the machine and immediately add the egg and water, taking about 5 seconds to pour it in. Process an additional 5 seconds. Scrape down the sides and bottom of the bowl to incorporate the flour more evenly., Process another 5 seconds. (Not all the flour will be incorporated.)

Empty the dough onto a flat work surface. Work in the remaining flour by using the heel of your hand to press and push the dough until it holds together. Shape the dough into a 6 inch disk. There should be many tiny flecks of butter and lard visible. Wrap the dough in plastic wrap or wax paper and refrigerate for at least 2 hours or overnight.

Variation: If Using Vegetable Shortening
For both the hand and the food processor methods, if using vegetable shortening instead of lard, cut in or process the butter alone until it is the size of large peas. Then add the vegetable shortening and either cut it in by hand or pulse several times to cut it into the flour. Proceed with the recipe as directed.

Milford Apple Pie

This pie is country comfort food, named after a small, friendly village in Ontario. Share this with good neighbours. Use a single unbaked prepared pie shell.

Filling:

1	**egg large**	***1***
1 cup	**sour cream**	***250 mL***
3/4 cup	**sugar**	***175 mL***
4 tbsp	**flour**	***65 mL***
dash	**salt**	***dash***
2 tsp	**vanilla**	***10 mL***
7	**Apples, peeled & cored**	***7***

Topping:

2 cups	**walnuts, chopped**	***500 mL***
1/2 cup	**white sugar**	***125 mL***
1/2 cup	**brown sugar**	***125 mL***
1/2 tsp	**salt**	***2 mL***
1 1/2 tsp	**cinnamon**	***7 mL***
2/3 cup	**flour**	***150 mL***
1/4 lb	**butter, melted**	***50 mL***
	frozen pie crust	

Beat egg, sour cream, sugar, flour, salt and vanilla together. Slice in Apples and mix. Pour into chilled pie crust and bake in preheated oven at 450 degrees F for 10 minutes. Lower heat to 350 degrees F and bake 25 minutes more. Take out of oven and cover with topping.

Mix walnuts, sugar, brown sugar, salt, cinnamon, flour, and melted butter together in a bowl and cover pie. Put pie back in oven at 350 degrees F for about 30 minutes or more until brown and done. Allow pie to set and cool.

Apple-Cranberry Pie

Before cranberry season is over, buy a couple of extra bags to stash in your freezer. Then you can bake this autumn pie any time of the year. Sprinkle the top crust with icing sugar, or use granulated sugar.

1 cup	**cranberries**	***250 mL***
3/4 cup	**sugar**	***175 mL***
2 tbsps	**Apple cider or pure apple juice**	***25 mL***
1 tbsp	**cornstarch**	***15 mL***
1/2 cup	**sugar**	***125 mL***
2 tbsps	**cornstarch**	***25 mL***
1/2 tsp	**cinnamon**	***2 mL***
1/2 tsp	**nutmeg**	***2 mL***
1 tsp	**finely shredded orange peel**	***5 mL***
5 cups	**Apples, peeled & thinly sliced**	***1.25 L***
	milk	
	sugar	
	double pie crust	

In a small saucepan combine cranberries, sugar, Apple cider, Apple juice, or orange juice, and cornstarch. Bring to boiling. Boil gently for 5 minutes, stirring frequently.

Cool 20 minutes. In a large mixing bowl combine sugar, cornstarch, cinnamon, nutmeg and orange peel. Add the Apples; toss to coat. Stir cooled cranberry mixture into Apple mixture. Transfer filling to pastry-lined pie plate. Place crust on filling. Seal, and crimp edge of pastry. Brush top crust with milk; sprinkle with sugar and cover loosely with foil. Bake in a preheated 375 degree F oven for 25 minutes. Remove foil and bake for 25-30 minutes more, or till top is golden. Cool.

The All-Canadian Ten Pound Apple Pie

This pie will feed two dozen people. Fantastic for family reunions, summer garden parties or to impress the office staff on pot-luck day. The cooking time is 2 to 2 1/2 hours. Cake pans that measure 14" x 17" are found in cookware or cake decorating stores. Make 2 batches of pastry for a double crust pie. You can make the pie a day ahead and reheat, or even freeze it. Choose a mixture of Cortlands, Spys and Idareds for this one.

1/4 cup	**lemon juice**	*50 mL*
10 lbs	**Apples**	*5 kg*
3 1/2 cups	**granulated sugar**	*875 mL*
1 1/4	**cups all-purpose flour**	*310 mL*
2 tsp	**ground cinnamon**	*10 mL*
1 tsp	**ground ginger**	*5 mL*
1/2 tsp	**ground nutmeg**	*2 mL*
1/2 tsp	**ground allspice**	*2 mL*
1 tbsp	**powdered sugar**	*15 mL*
1	**large egg yolk beaten with 2 tsp water**	*1*

In a large bowl mix lemon juice with 4 cups of water. Peel, core and slice Apples about 1/4" thick. As sliced, put Apples in bowl with water/lemon juice mix to slow browning. Drain Apples. Mix sugar, flour, cinnamon, ginger, nutmeg and allspice. Add this mixture to the apples, gently mix until all slices are coated.

Pour the Apples slices into a 2 inch deep 17 X 14" pan.

Make pastry (see page 180) lightly dust both sides of pastry with flour, then roll out on a well-floured board to make a topping 3 to 5 inches wider than pan. As you roll, occasionally check under pastry to make sure it is not sticking; dust with flour if it is. Slide a long spatula under pastry to release it if it sticks to the board.

Gently fold pastry into quarters. Support pastry with both hands to lift it off the board. Place it on the Apple filling with the tip of the triangle in the centre of the pan and unfold to cover the fruit.

Trim the pastry leaving 1 1/2 inches of overlap beyond the pan's rim. Fold the edge of the pastry under so it extends only about 1/2 inch over the rim, press pastry firmly against the pan's rim, fluting the edge. Slash the pastry's top decoratively. Brush the top of the pie with egg yolk mixture and sprinkle it with 1 tbsp of powdered sugar.

Set on the bottom oven rack. Bake at 375 degrees F, until the crust is well browned and the juices are bubbling (for 2 to 2 1/2 hours). The Apples in the centre should be tender when pierced. Check occasionally after 1 hour and cover with foil any part of the crust that is browned.

Set the pie on a rack and let it cool at least 2 hours; it will still be warm. If making ahead, let cool, cover and chill. To reheat it, lightly cover the pie with foil and bake in a 350 degree F oven until it's warm in the centre.

Serve the pie warm or cool. Cut into about 2 inch squares and use a spoon to scoop out the portions. Store leftovers in the refrigerator for up to 2 days.

Makes: 24 servings

Deep-Dish Caramel Apple Pie

Caramel-flavoured Apples combine deliciously with a crisp streusel topping. A bonus: There are plenty of juices from the pie to spoon over scoops of ice cream.

For streusel

3/4 cup	**all purpose flour**	***175 mL***
6 tbsp	**sugar**	***90 mL***
1 tsp	**pumpkin pie spice**	***5 mL***
1/4 tsp	**salt**	***1 mL***
6 tbsp	**chilled butter, cut into small pieces**	***90 mL***

For filling

3 lbs	**Apples (8), peeled, cored, cut into wedges**	***1.5 kg***
1/4 cup	**all purpose flour**	***50 mL***
1 1/4 cups	**sugar**	***310 mL***
1/4 cup	**plus 2 tbsp water**	***50 mL***
3 tbsp	**unsalted butter**	***45 mL***

Make streusel: Mix flour, sugar, pumpkin pie spice and salt in medium bowl to blend. Rub in butter with fingertips until mixture forms pea-size clumps.

Make filling: Combine Apple wedges and 1/4 cup flour in large bowl and toss to coat. Let stand while preparing caramel.

Stir sugar and 1/4 cup water in heavy large saucepan over medium heat until sugar dissolves. Increase heat and boil until syrup turns deep amber colour, swirling pan occasionally, about 5 minutes. Remove from heat. Add butter and remaining 2 tbsp water . Return to heat and stir until smooth. Pour caramel over Apples;

toss to coat. Let stand until Apples release juices, tossing occasionally, about 10 minutes. Spoon Apple mixture into a prepared pie crust shell. Sprinkle streusel over pie. Bake pie at 375 degrees F until Apples are tender and streusel is golden, covering crust edge with foil if browning too quickly. About 1 hour 10 minutes. Cool and serve.

Marinated Apple-Nut Pie

Some folks suggest not peeling the Apples or pears to retain their crunch and flavour. Use your favourite pie Apple.

4	**Apples (chunked)**	*4*
4	**Bartlett pears (chunked)**	*4*
1/2 cup	**shelled almonds**	*125 mL*
1/2 cup	**shelled filberts or hazelnuts**	*125 mL*
1/4 cup	**raisins**	*60 mL*
	cinnamon	
2	**Red Delicious Apples**	*2*

Mix first 5 ingredients together in a very large bowl. Sprinkle with cinnamon to taste. Let the mixture sit overnight in the refrigerator, partially covered (i.e. so that some air can circulate). The tips of the fruit may get brownish, but don't worry.

After marinating overnight, cut up the Red Delicious Apples and mix them in fresh. Then place in a pie crust and bake at 425 degrees for 25 to 35 minutes. Cool and serve.

Apple Cider Pie

An interesting twist, using spicy Apple cider as the liquid in the pie crust. Cortland, Spy or Idared for this one.

2 cups	**all purpose flour**	***500 mL***
1/2 tsp	**salt**	***2 mL***
2/3 cup	**shortening**	***160 ml***
6 tbsp	**Apple cider**	***100 ml***
2 cups	**Apple cider**	***500 mL***
6 inches	**cinnamon stick**	***6***
8 cups	**Apples, sliced, peeled, cooking**	***2 L***
1 tbsp	**lemon juice**	***15 mL***
1 cup	**dried mixed fruit bits or raisins**	***250 mL***
1/3 cup	**sugar**	***75 mL***
2 tbsp	**all purpose flour**	***25 mL***
3 tbsp	**butter**	***45 mL***
	milk	

Combine flour and salt. Cut in shortening until pieces are size of peas. Sprinkle 1 Tbsp cold Apple cider over part of mixture, toss with fork. Push side to side. Repeat until all is moistened (6 to 7 tbsp cider total); cover.

Bring the 2 cups cider with cinnamon stick to boiling. Boil gently, uncovered, for 20 minutes or until reduced to 1 cup. Strain through a cheesecloth-lined sieve. Discard cinnamon; set aside.

In saucepan, combine 2 tbsp cider mixture and Apples. Cook covered, 4 to 5 minutes or until tender, but not soft. Remove from heat. Add fruit bits; toss. Combine sugar and flour; stir into Apples.

Divide pastry in half. For bottom crust, on a lightly floured surface roll half of the dough into a 12 inch circle; fit into a 9 inch pie plate.

Trim pastry even with rim. Turn filling into pastry; dot with 1 tbsp butter. For top crust, roll remaining dough on floured surface into 12 inch circle. Make cutouts. Trim to 1/2 inch beyond edge. Seal and flute edge high. Brush with milk. Sprinkle with sugar. Cover edge of pie with foil.

Bake in a 375 degree F oven for 25 minutes. Remove foil; bake about 20 minutes more or until crust is golden. Cool. Serve pie with ice cream.

Notes:

Apple Cream Pie

1	**unbaked pie shell**	*1*
1 cup	**sugar**	*250 mL*
1/8 tsp	**salt**	*.5 mL*
1/2 cup	**flour**	*125 mL*
1 cup	**sour cream**	*250 mL*
1	**egg, slightly beaten**	*1*
1 tsp	**vanilla extract**	*500 mL*
2 cup	**Apples - finely chopped**	*500 mL*
1 tsp	**cinnamon**	*5 mL*
1/4 cup	**butter**	*50 mL*

Combine 2/3 cup sugar, 2 tbsp flour, and salt. Add sour cream, egg, and vanilla. Beat until smooth. Add Apples and pour into shell. Combine remaining flour, sugar, and cinnamon. Cut in butter. Sprinkle on top of filling and bake at 425 degrees F for 25-35 minutes. Cool and serve.

Notes:

Apple Custard Pie

For something a little out-of-the ordinary, try this decadent Apple custard combination. Drizzle a little maple syrup on each portion before you serve. Make sure there are large mugs of hot tea or coffee to accompany this rich dessert. Use the usual greats, Spy, Cortland or Idareds.

Crust:

1 1/2 cup	**flour**	***375 mL***
1/2 tsp	**salt**	***2 mL***
1/2 cup	**butter**	***125 mL***

Filling:

3	**Apples, peeled and sliced**	***3***
2/3 cup	**sugar**	***160 mL***
1 tsp	**cinnamon**	***15 mL***

Custard:

1	**egg**	***1***
1/2 cup	**sugar**	***125 mL***
1 cup	**evaporated milk**	***250 mL***

For crust, mix flour, salt and butter with a fork (or in food processor) until mixture resembles coarse meal. Press firmly on the bottom and sides of buttered pie plate. Place sliced Apples on crust, sprinkle with 2/3 cup of sugar and 1 tsp cinnamon. Bake at 375 degrees F for 20 minutes.

For custard: Beat egg, sugar and milk. Pour over Apples and return to oven for 30 minutes. Cool and serve.

Mile-High Apple Pecan Pie

Margaret Nuttal of Sarnia, Ontario, loves to cook when her family visits. Chock-full of Apples and crowned with a buttery pecan crumb topping, this dessert is queen in the Apple pie category. Use a prepared double pie crust.

Apple Filling		*12*
12	**Apples, peeled, cored, and sliced**	*250 mL*
1 cup	**sugar**	*25 mL*
2 tbsp	**flour**	*10 mL*
2 tsp	**cinnamon**	*10 mL*
2 tsp	**nutmeg**	*5 mL*
1 tsp	**vanilla extract**	

Butter Pecan Crumb		*250 mL*
1 cup	**all-purpose flour**	*80 mL*
1/3 cup	**sugar**	*1 mL*
1/4 tsp	**salt**	*125 mL*
1/2 cup	**butter, softened**	*125 mL*
1/2 cup	**chopped pecans**	
	Confectioners' sugar	
	prepared double pie crust	

In large pot over medium heat, cook apple slices until just tender and they give up their water-about 12 minutes. Remove from heat and drain well. Add sugar, flour, cinnamon, nutmeg, and vanilla; mix to blend and set aside.

In medium-size bowl, combine flour, sugar, and salt. Cut butter into flour mixture until coarsely blended. Add pecans and rub mixture briefly between fingers to form crumbs.

Heat oven to 375 degrees F. Fill pastry-lined pan with Apple filling, mounding in centre. Place second pie shell on top of filling to cover. Pinch edges of bottom and top crust together to seal.

Brush top of pie lightly with water and gently press crumb mixture on top. Cut several slits in top crust to vent steam; bake 45 to 50 minutes or until crust is golden brown. Cool at least 25 minutes. Sift confectioners' sugar over top and serve.

Piece-'Ah'-Cake Apple Orange Nut Pie

Try hard not to eat all the Apples raw. All the better with home-made marmalade but a tablespoon of Scotch will take an ordinary marmalade over the top. Sip slowly and don't drive your car.

	prepared double crust unbaked	
5 cups	**Apples, peeled, cored and chopped**	***1 L***
1 cup	**coarsely chopped pecans or walnuts**	***250 mL***
1/3 cup	**heaping orange marmalade**	***75 mL***
1 cup	**sugar**	***250 mL***
2 tbsp	**flour**	***25 mL***
1 tsp	**cinnamon**	***5 mL***

Mix all of the above in a big bowl. Place filling in unbaked pie crust, cover with second crust and bake at 375 degrees F for about 1 hour. Cool and serve.

New Elegance Apple Pie

The elegance is in the zest of the orange. A nice addition to a basic Apple pie. Guests will think you spent all day on this dessert. We won't tell them, if you don't.

	prepared double pie crust	
2 1/4 lbs	**Apples, peeled, cored, sliced**	*1.125 k*
3/4 cup	**sugar**	*175 mL*
2 tbsp	**all purpose flour**	*25 mL*
2 tbsp	**grated orange peel**	*25 mL*
2 tbsp	**Grand Marnier or other orange liqueur**	*25 mL*
3/4 tsp	**ground cinnamon**	*3 mL*
2 tbsp	**unsalted butter, cut into small pieces**	*25 mL*

Preheat to 400 degrees F. Place baking sheet on rack. Combine Apples, sugar, 2 tbsp flour, orange peel, Grand Marnier and cinnamon in large bowl; mix to blend well.

Spoon apple filling into pie crust-lined dish. Dot filling with butter. Arrange second crust over filling. Seal and crimp edges. Cut slits in top crust for steam vents.

Place pie on baking sheet in oven. Bake until crust is golden brown and apples are tender, about 50 minutes. Cool pie on rack at least 15 minutes. Serve warm or at room temperature.

Blue Moon Apple Pie

Don't get distracted by this very exciting pie crust, the filling takes you over the moon!

Crust:

1/2 cup	**butter or margarine**	***125 mL***
4 oz	**cream cheese**	***125 mL***
2 cups	**all-purpose flour**	***5 mL***

Filling:

2 1/2 cups	**Apples, peeled, cored & sliced**	***625 mL***
1 cup	**sugar**	***250 mL***
1/3 cup	**orange juice**	***75 mL***
2 tbsp	**honey**	***25 mL***
1/2 tsp	**cinnamon**	***2 mL***
1 tbsp	**all-purpose flour**	***15 mL***
1/2 cup	**butter or margarine**	***125 mL***

In a large bowl, combine butter and the cream cheese, and let sit until room temperature. Add flour, and blend well. Chill. Roll out half of the dough and place in a 9-inch pie plate. Reserve the remaining dough for the top crust.

In a saucepan, combine the Apples, sugar, orange juice, honey, cinnamon, 1 tbsp flour and butter and bring to a boil. Pour the mixture into the crust. Roll out the remaining crust and place over the filling. Cut slits in the top crust to allow steam to escape. Bake in a 350 degree F oven for 45 minutes.

Beverages

Always choose pure Apple juice
as others may include water,
flavourings or other additives.

'Cider' in Canada, means both 'hard' or
alcoholic cider and fresh pressed juice,
the choice is yours.

Honey Apple Shake

Milk shake enthusiasts will enjoy this twist. If you have some tall soda fountain glasses and long spoons, all the better!

4 cups	**chilled Apple cider or juice**	***1 L***
2 cups	**chilled orange juice**	***500 mL***
1/4 cups	**honey**	***50 mL***
2 tsp	**grated orange rind**	***10 mL***
1	**large scoop vanilla ice cream**	***1***
1	**large scoop Apple Ice (recipe page 152)**	***1***

Combine all ingredients and shake to blend. Pour into tall chilled glasses. Garnish with mint sprig, Apple slice or long peel of orange.

Makes 6 servings.

Notes:

Spiced Cider

Apres ski, apres hike, or apres snow shovelling, here is a ready-made cure for tired bones on a winter night.

8 cups	**Apple cider**	*2 L*
3 cups	**water**	*750 mL*
1/2 cup	**honey**	*125 mL*
6	**whole allspice berries or 1/2 tsp ground allspice**	*6*
3	**cinnamon sticks**	*3*
12	**cloves**	*12*
1/2 tsp	**ground nutmeg**	*2 mL*
1 cup	**lemon juice**	*250 mL*
1	**orange, sliced**	*1*

Bring Apple cider, water, honey, cinnamon, allspice, cloves, and nutmeg to a boil. Simmer for 30 minutes. Let stand overnight and then strain.

Add lemon juice and orange and reheat but do not boil. Can be put in a large coffee maker to keep warm.

Makes approximately 12 cups.

Notes:

Spicy Apple Brandy Cider

This spicy, potent beverage can be altered favourably by cutting back on the spices and when heating, drop in one whole orange, generously studded with whole cloves. Like Christmas, it's unforgettable.

8 cups	**Apple cider**	***2 L***
4	**whole cloves**	***4***
4	**whole allspice berries or**	***4***
	1/4 tsp ground allspice	
4	**whole cardamom seeds**	***4***
4	**cinnamon sticks**	***4***
1 cup	**Calvados or other Apple brandy**	***250 mL***

Combine cider or juice, cloves, allspice, cardamom and cinnamon sticks in a large saucepan. Simmer for 20 minutes; strain out spices and stir in Calvados or brandy.

Serve very hot in heavy mugs.

Makes approximately 9 cups

Notes:

The Great White North Slammer

Leave the vodka out of this 'Slammer' and you've got a terrific punch that the children will truly enjoy, summer, spring, winter and fall. Leave it in, and doctor it with drops of various liquers and just wait for the rave reviews from your guests.

2 cups	**pure Apple juice**	***500 mL***
1 12-oz can	**frozen cranberry juice cocktail concentrate**	***375 mL***
1 12-oz can	**frozen raspberry-cranberry juice cocktail concentrate**	***375 mL***
1 12-oz can	**frozen lemonade concentrate**	***375 mL***
1 liter	**bottle chilled ginger ale**	***1 L***
2 liter	**bottles chilled club soda**	***2 L***
1 cups	**cold water**	***250 mL***
3 cups	**chilled vodka**	***750 mL***

Combine frozen concentrates in a punch bowl. (A dutch oven or soup tureen makes a fairly suitable substitute.) Thaw, mix well and refrigerate until needed. At serving time, add ginger ale, club soda, water and vodka, if using.

Serve with plenty of ice. For a non-alcoholic version, add more club soda or juice to taste.

Notes:

Common Substitutions

Substitutions only work well under special conditions. Don't expect to get exactly the same results, but in a pinch, these will be suitable.

ALLSPICE:
1 tsp (5 mL) = 1/2 tsp cinnamon + 1/2 tsp ground cloves

BAKING POWDER:
1 tsp (5 mL) = 1/3 tsp baking soda + 1/2 tsp cream of tartar

BUTTERMILK: 1 cup (250 mL) = 1 cup yogurt or sour milk

CORNSTARCH
1 tbsp (15 mL) = 2 tbsp flour or 2 tbsp tapioca
= 1 tbsp arrowroot or 1 tbsp potato starch

CREAM:
Sour cream - 1 cup = 1/3 cup butter and 3/4 cup sour milk
Heavy cream 1 cup = 1/3 cup butter and 3/4 cup milk
Whipped - 2 cups = Chill one 385 mL can evaporated milk for 12 hours. Add 1 tsp lemon juice. Whip until stiff.

GARLIC: 1/8 tsp powder = 1 small clove

HERBS: 1 tbsp fresh = 1 tsp dried

MILK:
Sour - 1 cup = 1 cup milk minus 1 tbsp milk + 1 tbsp lemon juice or vinegar (let stand for 5 minutes)

SUGAR:
1 cup *granulated* = 1 cup corn syrup minus 1/4 cup other liquid as replacement for 1/2 the sugar in recipe or,
= 1 1/2 cup maple syrup minus 1/4 cup liquid
= 3/4 cup honey + 1/4 soda minus 3 tbsp liquid
= 1 1/3 cup molasses + 1/2 tsp soda minus 1/3 cup liquid
1 cup *brown* = 1 cup white minus 2 tbsp + 1/4 cup molasses. (Let stand one hour before using.)

index

D

T

V

W

A gift for any occasion

You can buy additional copies of *The Great Canadian Apple Cookbook* by completing the coupon below or sending us a note with your cheque or money order to:

Millview Publishing
Box 444
Bath, Ontario CANADA
K0H 1G0

Millview Publishing
The Great Canadian Apple Cookbook
P.O. Box 444
Bath, Ontario CANADA
K0H 1G0

Please send me _____ copy(ies) of ***The Great Canadian Apple Cookbook.***
Enclosed is $12.83 (includes $.84 GST) plus $2.00 postage and handling for each copy.

NAME ______________________________

ADDRESS ______________________________

CITY ________________ PROV ____________

POSTAL CODE ______________

Please allow 3 weeks for delivery.